THE BOOK OF
PALMISTRY

THIS IS A CARLTON BOOK

Text and design copyright © 1996 Carlton Books
Limited

First published in 1996 by Carlton Books Limited

10 9 8 7 6 5 4 3 2 1

A CIP record for this book is available from the
British Library

ISBN 1-85868-158-8 (hardback)
ISBN 1-85868-173-1 (paperback)

Project editor: Tessa Rose
Project art direction: Zoë Maggs
Design: Carol Wright
Production: Sarah Schuman

Printed and bound in Spain

Carlton Books Limited
20 St Anne's Court
Wardour Street
London W1V 3AW

This book is dedicated to:
Malcolm's granddaughter, Phoebe Heep;
Sasha's granddaughter, Anna Sophie Fenton;
and Sasha's young friend Simone Davis, who
is convinced, rightly, that Sasha hasn't grown
up herself yet.

ACKNOWLEDGEMENTS

As always, we owe a special debt to our
families, who gave us inspiration, encouragement and good cooked meals, not to mention
the liberty to use their hand prints. Especial
thanks to Jonathan Dee and his friends in
Cardiff; Martin Davis, his friends and family
in Scotland for prints and their innermost
secrets; and to Helen, Claire, Maria and
everyone else who contributed prints and
stories.

Most of all to our editor, Tessa Rose,
who has womanfully coped with heaps of
typescript, prints, illustrations and two totally
off-the-wall authors, all at breakneck speed
without once losing her sense of humour.

THE BOOK OF
PALMISTRY

How to Discover Success, Love & Happiness

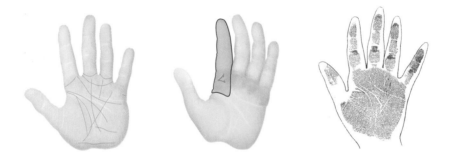

SASHA FENTON &
MALCOLM WRIGHT

CARLTON

CONTENTS

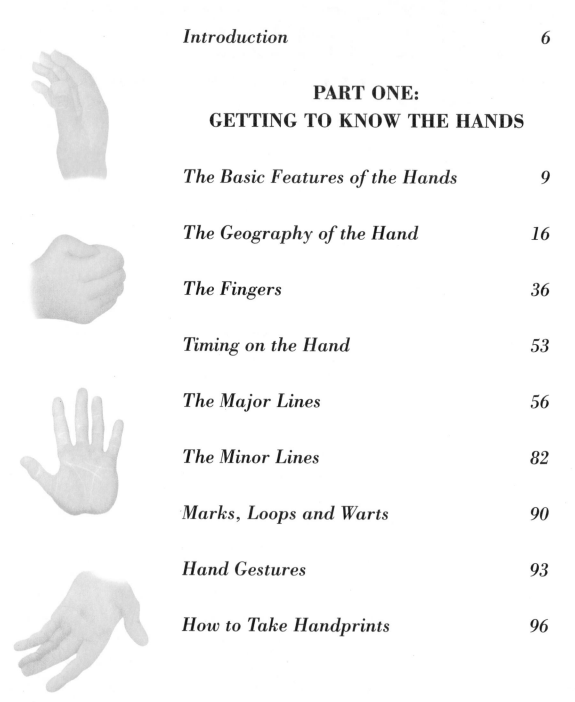

PART TWO:
READING ASPECTS OF OUR LIVES

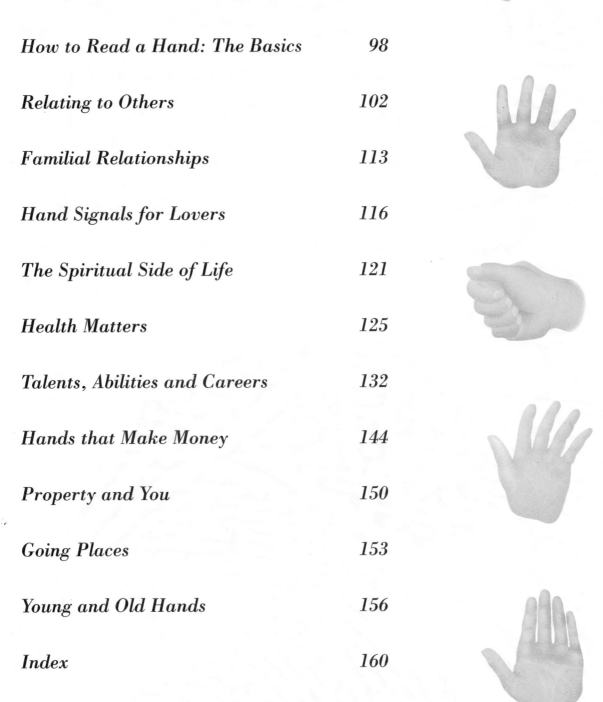

INTRODUCTION

*P*almistry falls into two component parts, one being character reading and the other ascertaining the events of the past, present and future. To some extent, it is hard to disentangle the two. This is because it is your own particular nature and your own special talents that combine with your ability to grasp opportunities or cope with setbacks. You can only fall deeply and passionately in love if you are a passionate person, and you can only become a top musician or sportsman if you are musical or sporty.

Most palmistry books concentrate on character reading because it is easier to describe and to understand than the techniques of prediction. In this book, we mix the two so that you can study your nature in addition to the way you respond to the fluctuations of your life. We have also deliberately mixed references to gender in the text, swapping from masculine to feminine and back again.

Everything about your hands, from their shape, the lines on your palms and the way you move them when talking, tells a tale about your character. Your fingernails, knuckles and even the heel of your hand all have plenty to say to a skilled palmist.

The symbol of a tree has been used in many religions to describe life unfolding from a seed. Such symbols range from the tree of life and the tree of knowledge to the human body itself, with the trunk as the spinal cord. So it is with palmistry. We can view the life line and the centre of the hand as the tree trunk, with the sap moving upwards to the fingers as branches and the fingertips as leaves. The top phalanges of the fingers describe the way you think and adapt to life, so it is up to you to work out when to grow new branches, put forth new leaves or to let old ones drop away. You can even allow yourself to rest for the winter if you so wish.

If you look on your palm as the trunk of a tree with the lines going up the palm as different ener-gies – physical, mental, emotional, spiritual, nervous and sexual – all having their job to do, you will see that palmistry is holistic, encompassing the mind, body and spirit of each person. If any of these lines or areas are blocked, the energy will go into the next one. For instance, if the sexual and emotional energies are switched off, you will pour your heart into work or some other interest or, alternatively, you may have a nervous breakdown. Balance is everything in palmistry as well as in life.

There are times when you can see extra energy being used in your life through the lines on your hands. If you want to look at this, just relax your hand, place it on a table and see if the little finger falls away from the others. If this is so, you are likely to be going through a restless period, wanting change and maybe to move forward in a different direction. If there are busy patches on the hand with many fine lines gathering together across the width of it, it is likely that at the ages at which the lines conjoin you will be very busy, probably doing too much and, hopefully, quite happy with your lot in life because of the productivity of the period.

Palmistry is not an easy skill to acquire, but whether you simply learn a bit of it for fun or begin to take the subject seriously, we guarantee that you will find yourself endlessly fascinated by it.

Sasha Fenton & Malcolm Wright, 1996

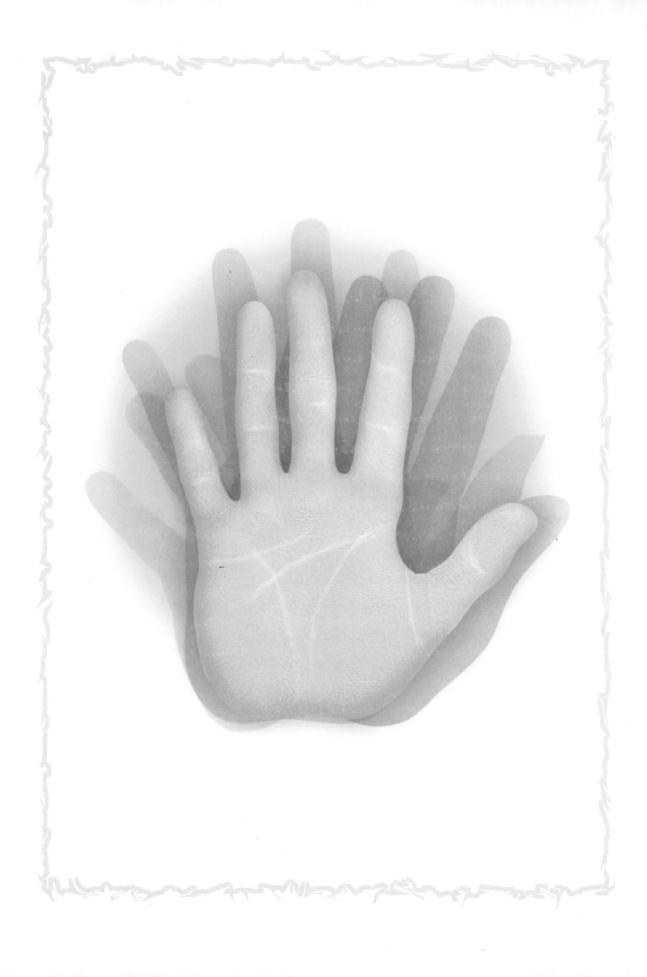

THE BASIC FEATURES OF THE HANDS

A *common question that is asked of us is, "Which hand do you read?" The answer is that we read both. Palmists have various theories about what can be seen on the right or left hands and there is some truth in most of these ideas. The first thing to establish is which is the dominant or major hand. This is the one we use most, especially when writing or using tools. In 90 per cent of the population this is the right hand, but many people use both hands. This seems to be more common in left-handed people, probably because they are forced to live in a right-handed world. It is worth asking ambidextrous people which hand they use for writing, using a screwdriver and so on.*

Major and minor

An experienced palmist can often spot the major hand without having to ask; in many cases, it is larger and it can be far less lined and creased than the minor hand. However, it is best to read both hands and to note the difference between them without worrying too much about which hand is giving you the information that you are seeking.

We have discovered that the minor hand tends to show those aspects of life that leave an emotional impact on people, while information on material matters and the practicalities of life are concentrated more heavily in the major hand. The minor hand is often more reliable when dealing with personal matters, such as the number of children that a person will have or the progress of a love relationship. The minor hand shows feelings, doubts, insecurities and those things that we try to hide from the world. The major hand tends to offer more information on such things as careers, money, travel and property.

Some palmists say that the minor hand shows what we want while the major one shows what we get. There is some truth in this because the major hand does tend to show how we adapt to the changes in our lives as they come along. The only theory that really doesn't work is that the minor hand looks backward while the major one looks forward. Both hands show events from the past and the future, though if an event in the past has left an emotional scar, this may show up more clearly in the minor hand.

To be honest, this theorizing is all very well but like so much in palmistry it doesn't always work! It can be hard enough to find the information that you want without worrying overmuch about which hand it comes from, so look at both of them.

PALM 🖑 WATCH

Think in terms of money, success, jobs and life in general when looking at the major hand and personal life when looking at the minor hand. However, don't take this advice too rigidly because hands are perverse and nothing can be taken for granted.

Hand sizes

We are governed by every part of our body, our height and our build. The shape of a subject's ears tells us a little about the type of music he likes, for instance, whether this is harsh or mellow: non-musical ears break up the sound before it enters the ear. Therefore our hands, which we use all the time, have a great influence on the way we act and think.

Generally speaking, people with larger hands go about things in a slow and methodical manner. They are likely to be good craftspeople, with a good eye for design

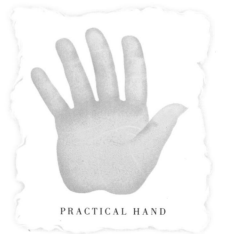

PRACTICAL HAND

and technical work. They hate to be rushed and can be extremely independent. These subjects may not always be practical and can be artistic and dreamy. People with long hands mature more slowly than those who have short hands and are unlikely to be risk-takers.

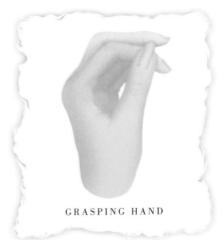

GRASPING HAND

If you want someone to come along and sort out your life, find a small-handed person – especially one with hands that are also somewhat square and practical-looking. These folk can throw a party for 50 people at the drop of a hat, sort out your computer, deal with a fractious child or animal and clear out a cupboard at the same time. They are often quite clever at making money, too.

Some very small-handed people are tight-fisted, crabby and selfish, but this depends upon the type of hand you are looking at as well as its size.

P A L M 🖐 W A T C H

If you happen to be musical, you may find this simple rule helpful. A subject who can press down a four-note chord on a piano using the octave has an average mentality, while those who can only manage less than an octave can be small-minded. A subject who can press down more than an octave has a broader mind.

Hand shapes

Many old-fashioned palmistry books describe the basic hand shapes as square, elementary, conic, spatulate, philosophical and psychic. None of these terms will mean much to a beginner and many professional palmists nowadays tend to apply common sense when making assessments of hand shapes rather than sticking to fixed principles. It is obvious, for example,

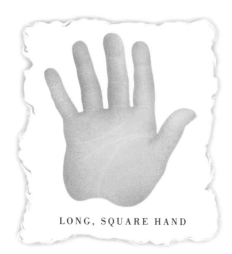

LONG, SQUARE HAND

that a square hand is more likely to belong to a practical person who works with his hands than an artistic or mystical type who is interested in creative or mystical matters; his hands will typically be long and narrow.

Variations on this theme will reveal that a person with a long, rather bony, square hand and a square palm is probably technically minded. Such a person might well work in computing, graphic arts or as an accountant (especially if the finger ends are also squared off).

Rounded hands belong to sociable people who need plenty of variety in their lives, while a longer, thinner hand belongs to a reflective, thoughtful type who needs time away from other people in order to work things through in his mind.

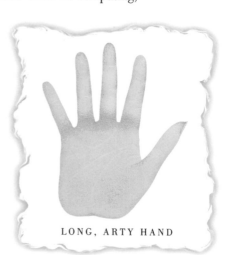

LONG, ARTY HAND

ROUNDED HAND

If the palms are fairly narrow at the wrist end but splay outwards towards the finger ends, the subject is inventive, independent and probably slightly eccentric. People with spatulate finger ends are convinced that only the best is good enough for them – but to do them justice, they will go out in the world and get what they want for themselves. If the heel of the hand is heavier and wider than the outer end, the indications are that the subject will have an interest in business, teaching or anything that brings both intellectual and material rewards.

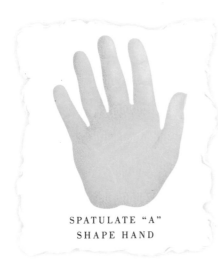

SPATULATE "A"
SHAPE HAND

Hands that look small, cramped and claw-like belong to cold-hearted, materialistic types. This is the type of person who can't wait for Aunty Annie to "pass over" because there may be a little some-thing – such as a house or two – left in a legacy for the subject! This type of subject often has hooked, claw-like fingernails that look as if they could scratch and grab at anything that comes near them (see page 11).

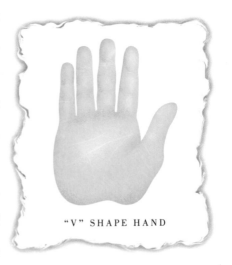

"V" SHAPE HAND

Small hands with hard-packed flesh suggest greed and selfishness, whereas large, fleshy hands can belong to a slow-moving and lazy type of person.

Soft hands can denote ill health; vegetarians also have softer than average hands. The kind of hand that feels like a wet flannel inside a polythene bag suggests a lazy person who allows others to run around after them. Hard or firm hands denote a hard-working person – look at the shape of the hand to discover whether this activity is mental or physical.

Knotted or bony hands denote a thoughtful person who doesn't rush into anything. These people are often hard workers and deep thinkers. Their nature is quite serious and they can worry quietly without telling others what is on their minds. They need to find an outlet for their creativity and to get involved in something they consider to be important. Some people who have small knotted hands never seem to get their lives into any kind of logical shape and spend their time yearning for what can never be. These knots are supposed to denote people who habitually take an orderly approach to every-thing they tackle, but there are plenty of disorganized people to be found with very knotty hands. This type of hand may often be seen on people who don't seem to have the mental or physical energy to make their lives work for them.

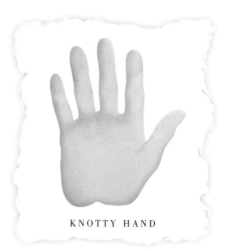

KNOTTY HAND

Full and empty hands

Some people's hands are full of lines while others have nothing more than the three basic lines of head, heart and life. Empty hands belong to simple folk whose lives are straightforward and free of complications. They can also denote a fairly happy-go-lucky person or someone who is never really going to do much with her life. Such people may be calm and peaceful or simply not willing to do more than is absolutely necessary.

Full-handed people are their own worst enemies because they fret and worry, often over nothing at all. They focus on their own feelings and may analyse themselves and their lives too deeply. Illness, insecurity and outside events will leave their mark on the hands. If a subject is being pushed around by others and cannot live her life in the way she wants, many lines of frustration and interference will show up. Outside influences also show up on such hands. A person who has very few lines simply doesn't take any notice of people or events that do not coincide with her own personal interests.

Lines come and go, especially the fine network of smaller ones, so the state of the hands really does reflect what is going on in a subject's life at the time of the reading. One needs to be careful here, because indications of illness and even the possibility of an early death can simply reflect the fact that the subject is totally fed up with her life at the time of the reading. The appearance of the hands will change again when the subject gets her life into some kind of shape.

The colour and general appearance of the hands

At one time palmistry books used to state that hairy hands belonged to uncouth people. It's still not uncommon to come across the idea of coarse-grained hands suggesting a coarse nature or fine-grained hands suggesting refinement. None of these notions stand close examination. Black and Indian people can have quite grainy hands and a large number of men from Mediterranean countries have hairy hands. To suggest that all these peoples are uncouth or coarse is ridiculous.

The colour of the hands depends to a great extent upon the health of the subject. Yellow hands on a European person suggest jaundice, while blue, grey or mauve ones suggest that the heart and lungs are not working properly or that there is something wrong with the circulation. Anaemia will make the hands cold and pale. If hands that are usually warm suddenly become cold (or vice versa), a health problem may be the cause. Thyroid problems, lung trouble and heavy smoking can make the hands red. The colour of the hands is relatively unimportant as long as it doesn't suddenly change. (Please turn to "Health Matters", pages 125–31, for more information on this.)

PALM WATCH

- Always read both hands. If you can't find the information you want on one hand, look at the other.
- Use common sense when judging hand shapes.
- Lines on the hand can come and go, especially the fine lines that you see on a "full" hand.
- The colour of the hands can vary between individuals and is usually only important if it changes.

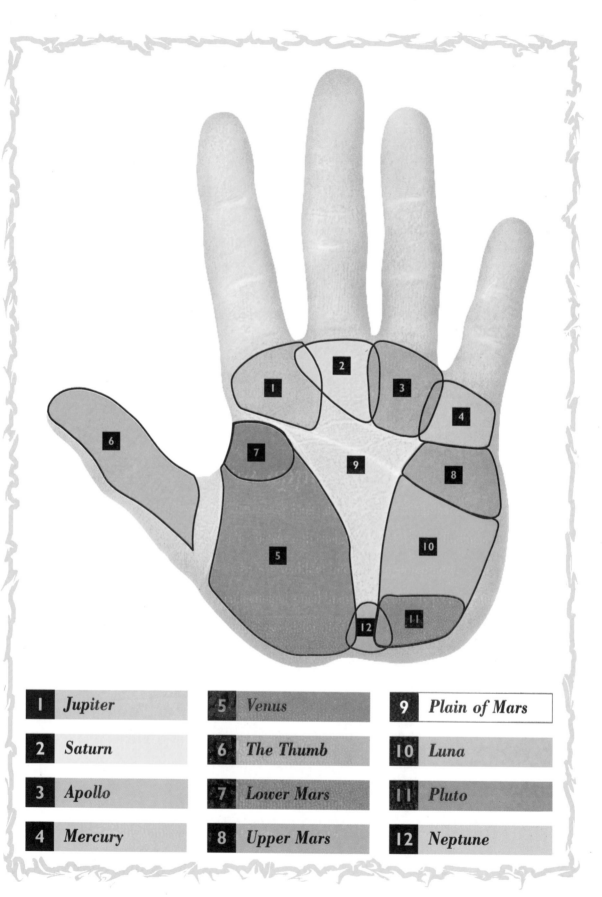

1 *Jupiter*		**5** *Venus*		**9** *Plain of Mars*	
2 *Saturn*		**6** *The Thumb*		**10** *Luna*	
3 *Apollo*		**7** *Lower Mars*		**11** *Pluto*	
4 *Mercury*		**8** *Upper Mars*		**12** *Neptune*	

THE GEOGRAPHY OF THE HAND

*T*o a palmist, the hand is a map that describes the nature of the person whose hand it is. All palmists learn their craft logically, getting to understand each area of the hand and then superimposing each line and mark. This is the art of palmistry – the ability to synthesize several items of information, often taken from different areas of the hand, at the same time. The beginner will not find this an easy concept to put into practice, so to simplify matters and avoid giving you an indigestible lump of disjointed information, we have divided the hand into areas. We have used a combination of topics within the various areas, or mounts, to help you decide what kind of person your subject is.

The mounts

The term "mounts" is understood by palmists the world over and refers to the various areas of the palm of the hand. The early hand readers who coined this expression also gave each of the areas a Roman planetary name; palmistry was closely linked to astrology at this time. The term is a bit of a misnomer, though, because many mounts are actually valleys.

One very important point that needs to be emphasized here is that old-time palmistry books and, unfortunately, some modern ones, suggest that these areas should be large, high and fairly free of lines and marks, except for specifically "lucky" ones, in order to ensure happiness, health and success in their corresponding areas of life. This is incorrect. In the first place, some of these areas cannot be high or large due to the anatomy of the average hand; secondly, a lack of lines or marks on these mounts may be a bad indication rather than a good one.

The sides of the hand

Palmists use the medical terms radial and ulna to describe the two sides of the hand. The radial or "outer" side is concerned with matters arising from living and working as a member of society. The ulna or "inner" side is concerned with the inner concepts of imagination, emotions, feelings and with travel (especially for pleasure).

The Jupiter Mount and Finger

This mount and its corresponding finger represent ambition, drive, salesmanship, leadership qualities and the desire to influence one's surroundings. A strong sense of self, complete with ambition, leadership qualities and idealism requires a long, straight Jupiter finger, backed by a firm and fairly full mount of Jupiter. Such people frequently wag their Jupiter fingers around as if they were lecturing others. A pointed Jupiter finger suggests strong moral views and a probable interest in religion or spiritual matters; this is especially so if the Saturn finger is long and rather pointy, too.

A high mount here with a long, strong Jupiter finger can indicate a fondness for teaching, but the real clincher is a square on the mount. If you look carefully to see where the lines that make up the square come from, you may even be able to work out the subjects that this person teaches.

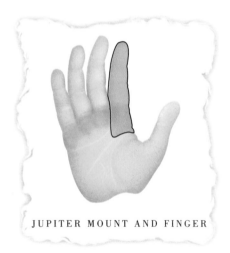

JUPITER MOUNT AND FINGER

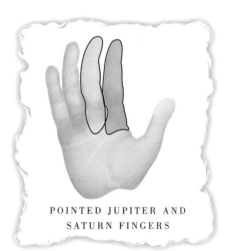

POINTED JUPITER AND
SATURN FINGERS

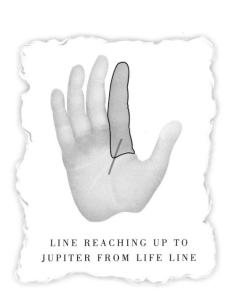

LINE REACHING UP TO
JUPITER FROM LIFE LINE

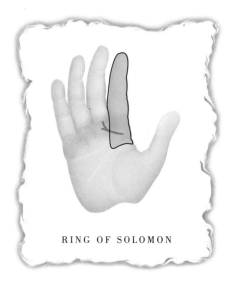

RING OF SOLOMON

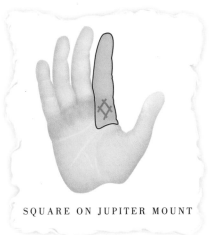

SQUARE ON JUPITER MOUNT

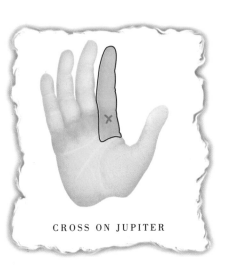

CROSS ON JUPITER

Lines and marks on Jupiter

If the life line appears to throw a darting line upwards to Jupiter, the subject is idealistic. Counselling ability is denoted by a line called the "ring of Solomon". Sometimes there are more than one of these rings. If the heart line throws a line or two into the mount of Jupiter, this indicates that the subject brings her ability to listen and to counsel into her personal relationships.

A square on the Jupiter mount can protect a subject from losses due to over-ambition. A cross on this mount is said to indicate that the subject will achieve her ambitions. This is especially so if the cross points up towards the Jupiter finger.

PALM ⚑ WATCH

◁ *Fingerprint types can be found on pages 46–7.*

◁ *A whorl fingerprint on the Jupiter finger makes the subject hard to influence. He won't want to listen to others or to trust their judgement.*

◁ *A peacock's eye or composite fingerprint on this finger denotes a gifted and adaptable personality. A double loop or double whorl denotes a subject who has the unusual ability of being able to mentally detach himself from what is going on around him and at times almost stand outside himself.*

The Saturn Mount and Finger

The term "mount" is a misnomer here because the area is usually flat or even slightly dipped. The Saturn finger is said to govern religious and moral views, scientific ability and a certain dourness or Saturnian aspect to the character. If the finger is particularly long, therefore, it might indicate the kind of mind that turns to religion, science or detailed research. A square end to this finger adds accountancy ability, while a

SATURN MOUNT AND FINGER

large, square fingernail adds the ability to concentrate on detailed work, possibly of a creative kind.

Lines and marks on Saturn

Practically everybody has some lines that run upwards to the Saturn finger, and these have a number of probable meanings. One is that the subject may work hard throughout his life and he will earn the money he needs and

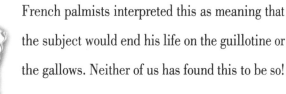
wants as a result. However, such lines can indicate inherited money that has accrued as the result of other people's prudence. This is especially so if there is a line from inside the life line reaching towards Saturn. Either way, lines that run upwards to Saturn are a good indication of being well provided for later in life, wherever that provision originates from. Many lines on this mount suggest a number of sources of income.

FATE LINE ON SATURN

A cross or some other barrier to the flow of energy in this area may indicate a temporary financial problem. Long ago French palmists interpreted this as meaning that the subject would end his life on the guillotine or the gallows. Neither of us has found this to be so!

The Apollo Mount

There may be a mount somewhere under this finger, but it is often set to one side, with the lines running alongside it. Just consider this to be the Apollo area and don't worry about whether it is

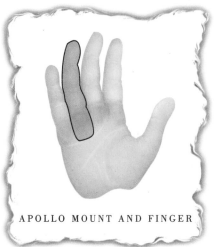

APOLLO MOUNT AND FINGER

really a mount at all. The finger and Apollo area are associated with a number of pleasant things, including home or family life, creativity, artistic talent and fun.

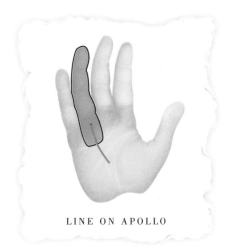

LINE ON APOLLO

Lines on Apollo

An Apollo line (or group of lines) is supposed to denote fame and fortune, but we haven't found this to be the case. Many ordinary people have one, whereas famous people may or may not. However, it is an indication of a creative person who finds more to enjoy in life than work and money. If the line is strong at the top of the palm on the mount, the subject will achieve merit through his own talent, especially in the arts.

The start of an Apollo line can give some indication of the time in life when a subject will settle down in a home of his own.

The presence of a line or a number of lines leading up over the Apollo mount to the Apollo finger is always a good sign. Such lines suggest that the subject will be happily settled later in life, the strength and condition of the lines indicating the amount of joy that can be expected. If these lines fade or disappear before reaching the finger, it is worth warning the subject not to use her home as a guarantee for any business scheme because there is a real chance of loss.

Islands (see page 91) on this line, as on any other line, show doubt, confusion and possible loss. Alternatively, if the line is strong, well defined and extending from the heart line up to the finger, the subject's domestic situation will be happy and secure, especially later in life.

A line that splits into a "V" here shows that the subject is likely to take

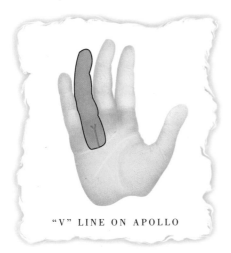

"V" LINE ON APOLLO

care of his parents later on, either by living with them or by taking an interest in their welfare.

A line that creeps across the hand from close to where the life and head line begin and turns upwards to end as part of the collection of lines on the Apollo mount is always interesting. This indicates that the subject will inherit either property or money that she subsequently spends on property. If you suspect this is showing up on your subject's hand, check with the family line and the fate line, too, as indicated in the property section (see pages 150–2). A strong additional line in this area can indicate a second property, a holiday home, a time-share or even a caravan. However, the family lines and the fate line will need investigating to confirm this. Changes in the Apollo line suggest moves of house, domestic upheavals or similar.

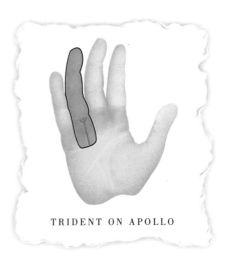

TRIDENT ON APOLLO

A trident on Apollo shows that the subject will never be without money and will always have a home.

The Apollo Finger

If the Apollo finger is long – that is, longer than the Jupiter finger – the subject has strong creative and artistic talents. If the finger end splays outwards, there will be a love of music. A droplet on the fingertip suggests a talent for practical arts and crafts. Cooking and gardening could come into this category, as could dressmaking or pottery.

If this finger is almost as long as the Saturn finger, the subject is likely to make a career in a creative or artistic field of endeavour.

When this finger is long and the Apollo line is present, there is a certain amount of vulnerability connected to the heart. (It is possible that disease or weakness will be present, but this is a complicated matter which we will look at more closely in the chapter on health, see pages 125–31.) These characteristics together with a long and curving heart line denote a romantic person who can be badly hurt.

PALM ✋ WATCH

◁ A strong Apollo finger and mount with a whorl fingerprint denotes that anything the subject has got has come through her own efforts. In short, that she is a self-motivator and a high achiever. In a relationship this type of person sets the emotional standards and makes the rules, and then moves the goalposts without telling a soul. (If you meet anyone like this, it is worth finding out whether she has a strong Scorpio influence on her horoscope.)

◁ A composite or peacock's eye fingerprint on the Apollo finger suggests that the subject is creative, especially in arts and crafts, and could well be self-taught. Such people are self-motivated and achievers. They are self-sufficient and possess such tremendous inner resources that if they were to retire they would soon be as busy with their own interests as they were with their career, or even busier.

◁ There are many parts of the hand that give clues to the state of a subject's relationships and these will be dealt with later (see pages 102–12), but here is one that can be seen on the Apollo mount. When the line doubles on the Apollo mount, the subject and his partner could be happy in later life as long as they each have their own interests.

The Mercury Mount and Finger

This area of the hand concerns communication and relationships, and there is a great deal of information to be found here. Much of this is covered in the love and relationship section – see pages 102–12.

MERCURY MOUNT
AND FINGER

The length and width of the Mercury finger can tell us a lot about a person's ability to communicate. Experience will soon show you what is an average Mercury finger. Basically, the finger should look right for the size and shape of the hand. If this is the case the person will be able to communicate with others at work and elsewhere in the normal way. If the finger is either particularly short or thick or unusually long or thin, there may be some kind of mental problem.

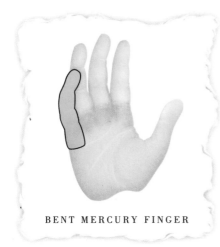

BENT MERCURY FINGER

From time to time you may come across a Mercury finger that is bent over or oddly shaped. This may simply be an inherited feature and not be significant. However, we have come across this type of Mercury finger in people who become deaf in later life, or who are so stubborn and unwilling to listen that they literally "don't hear" what others are telling them.

Marks on Mercury

A cross on Mercury denotes that the subject is comfortable operating machinery that is used for his job. This is most commonly seen in people who use communications equipment, thus computer users, accounting personnel and telephonists often have such a mark. We have also come across

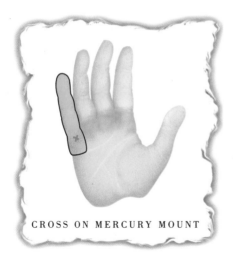

CROSS ON MERCURY MOUNT

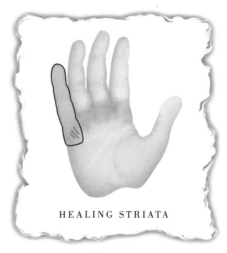

HEALING STRIATA

catering workers, engineers and motor mechanics with similar marks.

In Roman mythology, the god Mercury ruled medicine. His symbol was the caduceus, the winged staff with a snake entwined around it, a symbol still associated with medicine today. Anyone who works in any kind of healing capacity has healing striata, this includes professional or amateur counsellors and even beauty therapists. Oddly, this mark is so precise that it cannot be taken for anything else, and that is a very unusual situation in palmistry. Stranger still, this healing mark looks a bit like the stem of the caduceus symbol itself.

Another indication of a healer, listener, carer or even a good family

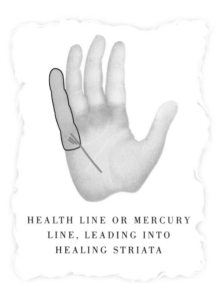

HEALTH LINE OR MERCURY
LINE, LEADING INTO
HEALING STRIATA

person is a line of health or Mercury line that leads up to the area of – and frequently into – the healing striata. The Mercury or health line also gives some indication of a spiritual pathway or purpose in life (see pages 121–4).

A small fan-shaped mark just above the heart line and at the base of the Mercury mount is often found in those who enjoy helping and advising the public but who are not directly involved in the business of healing. Such people can be found in shops, information booths, Citizens' Advice Bureaux, the police, and even sitting at a supermarket checkout or receiving your library books. They understand the needs of others.

PUBLIC HELPER MARK

P A L M 🖐 W A T C H

⬥ *A strong branch line coming off the fate line and ending up in the area between the mounts of Mercury and Apollo denotes that the subject has a good chance of getting something published.*

⬥ *If there is a whorl on the Mercury finger the subject gets bored with others fairly quickly. Such a person may be successful in journalism or sales.*

The Mount of Upper Mars

This can look like a mount but it may be quite flat. The area is associated with the idea of energy of various kinds – for example, the fight-or-flight response, the energy to argue a point or to get things done.

Feel your subject's percussion area with your fingers. If it is thick through to the back of the hand, your subject is a fighter. The urge to fight could make him a boxer, wrestler or a soldier, but he could simply be a tough person who battles for what he wants or for what he thinks is

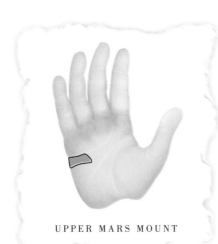

UPPER MARS MOUNT

right. A very high mount belongs to someone with a very short fuse and a violent temper.

A reasonably thick Mars mount denotes a subject who is fairly unshockable. It can also suggest someone who works with his hands for a living. A subject with a thin Mars mount denotes an opposite type, someone who works with his mind and is easily upset or shocked by events.

MERCURY/HEALTH LINE AND
CURVED LINE OF INTUITION

Lines on Mars

If a health line, a line of Mercury or a curving line of intuition passes by this mount, the subject may fight for the rights and needs of others. Alternatively, he may even fight to keep someone alive and well. This line refines the Mars area, suggesting an interest in health or spiritual matters rather than actual combat.

There is also a line, commonly seen, that enters the hand from the percussion edge on Mars and ends up joining the Apollo lines. This means that the subject is a hard worker. It can also show that foreigners or foreign places figure strongly in his life.

(Travel lines can be seen on the percussion side of Mars – see the illustration on page 30 and pages 153–5.)

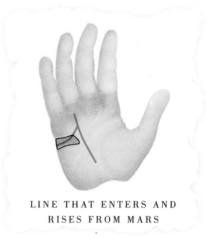

LINE THAT ENTERS AND
RISES FROM MARS

The Mount of Luna

Luna lies directly opposite the mount of Venus. This juxtaposition is telling: if you think of Venus as being associated with goods, possessions,

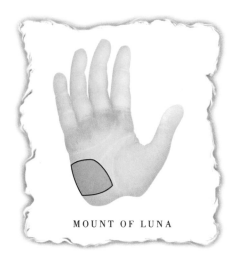

MOUNT OF LUNA

money and anything that can be appreciated by the senses, you will quickly grasp the idea that Luna is concerned with the non-material aspects of life, the things you cannot see, feel and touch; such as the imagination, experiences, emotions and creativity. Spiritual and intellectual matters can also be seen on the mount of Luna.

If this mount is large, wide, full or high, the subject needs plenty to think about and opportunities to exercise his imagination. This subject may be a traveller, an intellectual, a poet, or an artist. A high mount may also indicate psychic ability – see pages 121–4. Material goods may not be of interest, but if the well-developed Luna is balanced by an equally full Venus, the chances are that he wants the fun, the experiences and the money!

A well-defined Luna suggests a caring and charitable nature with time for the needs of others.

Lines on Luna

If any lines entering the hand from the percussion side drift across Luna to touch the life line, the mount of Venus or any other part of the lower palm, there will be strong attachments to other countries and other places. This can mean that the subject will live overseas for a period, but you will have to check the life, fate and Apollo lines

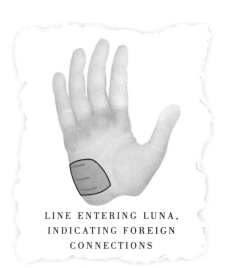

LINE ENTERING LUNA, INDICATING FOREIGN CONNECTIONS

for more information on this. (See pages 153–5 for more on travel.)

A head line that curves downwards into Luna denotes a creative or imaginative person; the deeper the curve, the greater the imagination.

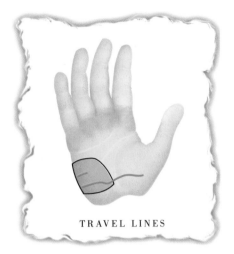

TRAVEL LINES

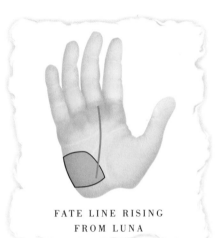

FATE LINE RISING
FROM LUNA

Forks on the head line indicate writing or communication ability, and if one fork falls downwards towards Luna, the subject could be a creative story teller (or maybe a bit of a liar).

Palmistry books used to tell us that a head line that dips down too far into Luna suggests suicidal tendencies. There is some truth in this, because such a person can become overwhelmed by his feelings and take things to extremes. A fork in the head line that dips into Luna can suggest a creative imagination or an unpractical streak. A straight upper fork will help to balance the over-imaginative aspect of such a nature.

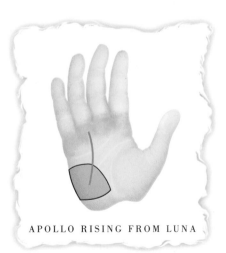

APOLLO RISING FROM LUNA

If the fate line starts on Luna, help will be given by outsiders at the start of the subject's career. There is an old theory that such a subject will be valued by outsiders rather than by his family.

In some cases the Apollo line rises from Luna and this may suggest that the subject has a home of his own from an early age. It can also indicate early fame and fortune as a result of the subject's creativity.

LUNA TRAVEL

Palmistry theory books will tell you that travel is shown on the mount of Luna. This idea is taken from ancient astrology and the notion of the Moon moving around much more quickly than the planets. The ancients also thought that the Moon disappeared into the sea whenever it wasn't visible in the sky.

The main problem with this theory for palmists is that it is often difficult to work out precisely where Mars ends and Luna begins. Travel lines appear all the way down the percussion side, from the heart line to the wrist. We will look at these in more detail later – see pages 153–5.

The Mount of Pluto

This mount is found at the base of Luna and it seems to denote restlessness and a desire for travel. Hidden away at the heel of the hand, it may carry information on a subject's underlying feelings and emotions. A mount that dips down towards the wrist suggests that the subject can recover from disasters and reconstruct his life when necessary.

MOUNT OF PLUTO

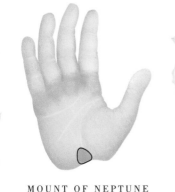

MOUNT OF NEPTUNE

The Mount of Neptune

This is the bridge area between the materialism of Venus and the imagination of Luna. If there is a dip rather than a bridge, the subject may find

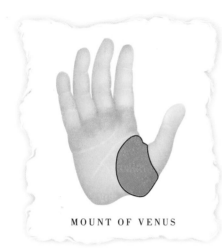

MOUNT OF VENUS

it hard to balance these aspects, favouring one over the other. If this mount connects the two adjacent mounts, there is a blend of creativity, charitable behaviour, thoughtfulness, adventurousness, psychic ability and materialism.

The Mount of Venus

Oddly enough, for such a large area of the palm there is not much information to give. We think that the key idea behind this mount is ownership and/or the desire for material possessions. In short, those goods, resources, finances, properties, possessions and luxuries that the subject values and appreciates. A new fitted kitchen would be a Venus matter, because it can be shown to one's friends and neighbours. Holiday snaps can also be shown but the experience of a journey can only be described, hence this would be a Luna matter.

Large, high Venus mount

A high Venus mount certainly shows the desire for worldly goods while not guaranteeing that the subject will actually obtain them! He is more likely to succeed in this respect if the Jupiter mount is also high, because this is found in those who will go all out for what they want.

A large, high mount of Venus indicates tremendous sexuality – or so state all other palmistry books. In our opinion, this is not the whole story. A large, full Venus belongs on the hand of someone who has great energy and a desire to live life to the full. He may work hard, enjoy his sports, hobbies and interests and be enthusiastic about his family. A full Venus belongs to someone who enjoys food, drink, art, music, gardens, comfort, warmth, laughter, nice clothes and much more. He likes the company of attractive people and he gets pleasure from all manner of things that feel and smell good – including sex!

If the mount is high, he may work with his hands in a practical field, such as engineering or farming. A flatter mount will suggest a type of work requiring brain rather than brawn.

Small, flat Venus mount

A small, cramped Venus suggests some level of poverty. If this area is less cramped at the wrist end, the situation is likely to improve later in life. If the area is small and flat, the subject's values may be spiritual rather than materialistic. If the whole area is cramped, the subject may never have much luck with money or resources. Such people obtain things only to lose them again later on; others never get them in the first place, or never want them.

It doesn't follow that a person with a small or flat mount has no interest in sex. He or she can be quite sensual and sexual, but is much more controlled and less rumbustious about it than someone with a full mount. A narrow Venus denotes a lazy lover who lies back and allows his (or her) partner to do most of the work in bed. It can also indicate a person who detaches himself (or herself) emotionally from the act of sex. What this subject does, feels and thinks can all be very different things! A reasonably sized but flattish mount belongs to a sexual technician who enjoys giving pleasure as well as receiving it.

Where a small or flat mount is found an aesthetic attitude may prevail. Alternatively, the subject may be undemanding. However, such people can make demands on others by their very weakness, complaining and whining when they don't get their way. A flat mount suggests a gentle non-pushy disposition.

Lines on Venus

The line that runs around the base of the thumb is known as the family line. Two family lines can indicate that there are two properties within the family. If this line becomes red or blue, it shows that the subject is worrying about his family.

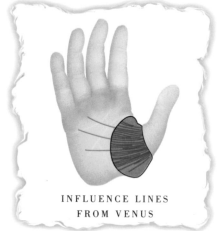

INFLUENCE LINES
FROM VENUS

Lines that radiate out from this area across the hand can indicate interference from or worry about family members. These problems can be dated by where they cross the life line (see page 53). The end position of these lines can show what they affect. For example, lines that touch the heart line can show family interference in a subject's love life. Some palmists see these lines as indicating new relationships entering a subject's life and date these from the time and place at which they cross the life line, but we are not so sure about this.

Extra life lines or lines that are behind the life line on Venus can indicate backing from the family. In some cases, this is spiritual backing that comes from family members who have died! Lines that enter Venus from the heel of the thumb area can indicate help from friends.

Forward or backward thinking?

There is often a deep crease that crosses Venus from the thumb area and runs across the hand. If this crease runs upwards, the subject tends to live in the past; if it runs downwards, he lives in the future.

CREASE

MOUNT OF LOWER MARS

The Mount of Lower Mars

If this area is full the person enjoys being part of a team and is cooperative in group activities. This is especially so if the fingerprints carry loop skin ridge patterns. A line here shows the kind of person who enjoyed being a boy scout, girl guide or something similar as a child. This line would also indicate if the subject enjoyed a period of time in community service or the armed forces.

The Thumb

The thumb shows whether the subject is logical and if she has a strong will. The knuckle at the base of the thumb shows organizational ability. The angle at the join of the heel of the hand to the wrist shows whether she has a sense of rhythm or not. (You will find more about this in the chapter on fingers, see pages 49–51.)

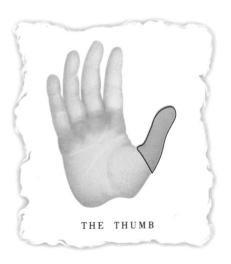

THE THUMB

The Plain of Mars

This is just the middle of the hand where many lines converge. The area doesn't seem to have any character of its own and nothing of significance is associated with it. There are many lines and marks that pass through this area or are to be found independently on it, but these will be covered between pages 57 and 91. If the palm is "hollow" here, the subject likes money.

PART ONE

THE FINGERS

*E*ach finger represents a different aspect of a subject's character. There are various ways of measuring fingers to work out whether they are long or short. Most palmistry books suggest that the fingers should be as long as the palm, but palms vary tremendously so this doesn't really work. We suggest that you just look at your subject's hand and make up your own mind as to whether the fingers are long, short or average. The art of palmistry is knowing what the happy medium is and when something is greater or lesser than this.

Length and thickness of fingers

Long fingers belong on the hand of an artistic or spiritual person who spends a lot of time thinking. These people don't like to be rushed: they go at their own pace but find it easy to cope with details. Short-fingered people see the grand design but have little patience for details. If you have a party and you want help in the kitchen, it is all your short-fingered pals who will get stuck into the job. They are quick and practical. If the fingers are thick as well as short, they may live in a mess, because they don't have the patience to tidy up.

Thick-fingered folk don't waste any time

SHORT AND LONG FINGERS

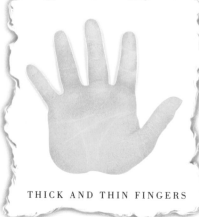

THICK AND THIN FINGERS

but jump in and get the job done. They have no patience with those whom they consider to be fools and they can be tactless, but they are direct and honest. Thin fingers belong to discreet, diplomatic people who care what others think. They are also precise, logical, thoughtful and patient. These subjects can be sarcastic when under pressure.

Knotted fingers

Subjects with knobbly knuckles don't take chances with their lives but prefer safety and security. Most knots only appear on the middle knuckles and these are called knots of material order. They endow their subject with an organized approach to life. Knots of mental order are found on the joints next to the fingertips and these denote an organized mind. Someone who has long, knotted fingers enjoys research projects and has the ability to bring several strands together in an organized manner.

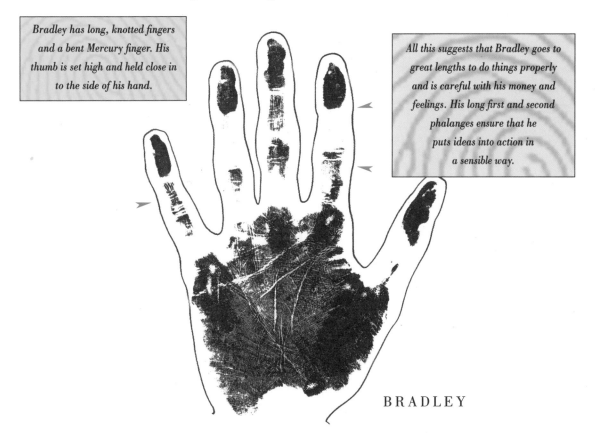

Bradley has long, knotted fingers and a bent Mercury finger. His thumb is set high and held close in to the side of his hand.

All this suggests that Bradley goes to great lengths to do things properly and is careful with his money and feelings. His long first and second phalanges ensure that he puts ideas into action in a sensible way.

BRADLEY

Setting

Fingers are set on hands in various ways – they can sit in a nice neat row at the top of the palm, slope down from the index to the little finger or form an arc. This makes it hard to work out the relative lengths of the fingers. If you enjoy being precise you can measure each finger, but if you don't want to be that thorough at this stage, just use common sense when judging them.

SETTING

OPEN AND CLOSED HANDS

The way the fingers lean

Fingers can be splayed out, close together or leaning towards one another. Splayed fingers suggest an open, honest nature with a tendency to spend money freely. These people may find family life stifling. Slight gaps between fingers suggest a reasonable subject who is open to ideas from others. Those who keep their fingers tightly together may not listen to what others have to say and they can be tight-fisted or afraid of spending money. Those whose fingers all lean inwards towards each other need to have their family around them.

The Characteristics of the Fingers

We have already looked at the fingers in conjunction with the mounts they are associated with in the preceding chapter. In this section we will explore their key characteristics and provide a rundown of the meanings attached to the way they lean.

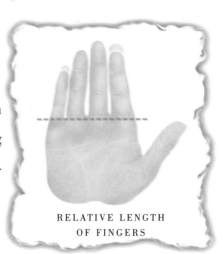

RELATIVE LENGTH OF FINGERS

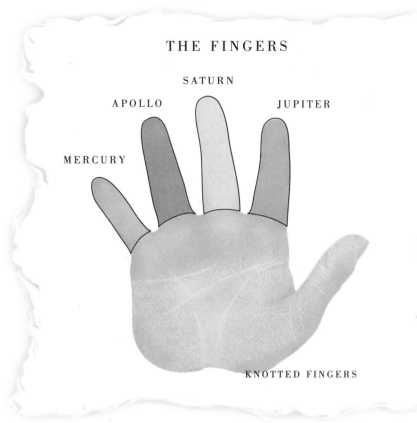

THE FINGERS

SATURN

APOLLO

JUPITER

MERCURY

KNOTTED FINGERS

Jupiter finger

This is related to the ego, leadership qualities, personal, religious and moral views and idealism. This finger governs the things that the subject believes in and whether he keeps those views to himself or seeks to influence others. Remember that when running through the relative lengths of the fingers, their setting on the hand can make them appear to be longer or shorter than they actually are. If you are in doubt, measure them and compare their length against each other. A long Jupiter finger is longer than the Apollo finger and not far short of the Saturn finger.

The Saturn finger

This finger represents the practicalities of day-to-day life and is concerned with money, resources and security. It is also connected with land, property, farming and earning power. A normal Saturn finger denotes the ability to study and to cope with technical or scientific concepts. Religious observance (or otherwise) is associated with this finger.

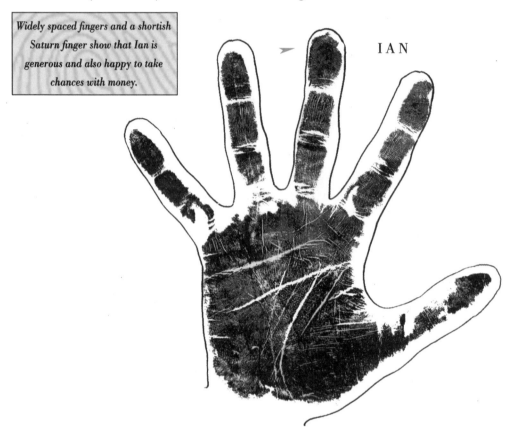

Widely spaced fingers and a shortish Saturn finger show that Ian is generous and also happy to take chances with money.

IAN

The Apollo finger

This finger is associated with love of a particularly pure and innocent kind as well as the pleasure and enjoyment of a home and family. Hobbies, artistic and creative pursuits, gambling, holidays and the pleasures of life are associated with this pleasant and dreamy finger. In many countries this finger (on either hand) is associated with marriage, engagement or romantic commitment.

The Mercury finger

This finger is associated with communication of all kinds, especially the ability to talk and to write. Sexual matters and sexual communication are associated with this finger. It is the hardest to measure because it is likely to be set lower than the others. However, if it reaches up to the top joint on the Apollo finger, you can consider it to be long.

Inclination

The way fingers lean towards or away from each other can reveal a great deal about a person. The principal ideas connected with each type of inclination are shown in the tables below. Look at the inclination of each finger and note the implication it carries for the fingers either side of it.

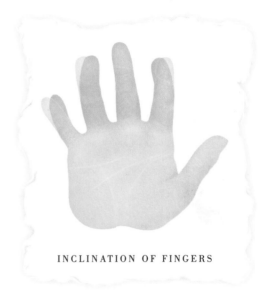

INCLINATION OF FINGERS

JUPITER FINGER

OUTWARDS – AWAY FROM SATURN	TOWARDS SATURN
Independent	*Persistent hard worker*
Materialistic	*Ambitious*
Dynamic	*Emotionally vulnerable*
Ambitious	*Fears hurt and rejection*

SATURN FINGER

TOWARDS JUPITER	TOWARDS APOLLO
Restless	*Writing skills*
Competitive	*Family pressures make the subject work hard*
Controlled or inhibited emotionally	

APOLLO FINGER

TOWARDS SATURN

Could be psychic

Prefers work to domestic tasks

Clever

Logical

Rational

TOWARDS MERCURY

Rebellious

Unusual

Literary and artistic talent possible

Could write songs

MERCURY FINGER

TOWARDS APOLLO

Sympathetic

Has counselling ability

Shrewd in business and/or sales

Mainly optimistic, can be irritable when under pressure

LEANING OUTWARDS

Lacks confidence

Doesn't want to go it alone

Needs encouragement

May keep others at an emotional distance or be unlucky in love

Length and Setting

Long and short fingers each have their own characteristics and the setting of

each finger can be important too.

LENGTH AND SETTING

FINGER	LONG	SHORT	HIGH SET	LOW SET
JUPITER	*Ambitious*	*Shy*	*Confident*	*Lacks courage*
	Self-centred	*Loving*	*Outgoing*	*Indecisive*
	A leader	*Warm*	*Opinionated*	*Martyr*
	Money-minded	*Insecure*		

LENGTH AND SETTING (cont)

FINGER	LONG	SHORT	HIGH SET	LOW SET
SATURN	Studious	A gambler	Should always be high set	Mentally abnormal
	Scientific	Either lucky or a waster		
	Religious			
	Pessimist			
APOLLO	Nice manners	Practical	Artistic	May not care for art or music
	Impractical	Realistic	Flamboyant	
	Artistic			
MERCURY	Good talker	Shy	Good at sales	Shy
	Good writer	Inarticulate	Outgoing	Inarticulate
	Friendly	Sexually peculiar/ repressed	Dexterous	Clumsy
	Sexy			

THE SECTIONS OF THE FINGERS

Phalanges

The phalanges are the three sections of each finger. Technically speaking, the singular of this is a phalanx and the plural phalanges. However, most palmists call each of these a phalange, so we shall follow the traditional pattern. Thick phalanges show energy and enterprise but they can also denote a coarse side to the nature. Thin phalanges show more refinement but a weaker and more nervous attitude.

THE PHALANGES

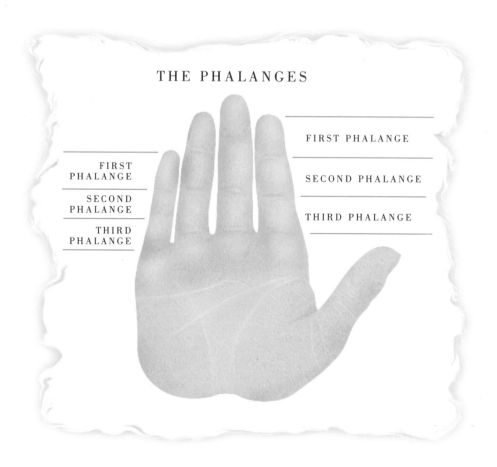

FIRST PHALANGE

SECOND PHALANGE

THIRD PHALANGE

FIRST PHALANGE

SECOND PHALANGE

THIRD PHALANGE

THE PHALANGES AT A GLANCE

	FIRST	SECOND	THIRD
LONG	Mentally active	Puts ideas into action – gardener, cook etc.	Good builder
	Likes maths, crosswords, computing	Could be good with hands – artistic, teacher etc., depending on which finger	Healthy appetite for food, sex, life
	Spiritual rather than materialistic		If fat, a glutton
SHORT	Mentally lazy	Lazy	Physically weak
	Can't grasp new ideas	Ignorant	Won't make an effort
	Materialistic	Unwilling to make an effort	If fat, greedy
	Suspicious of others		

PALM ✋ WATCH

◢ *The first phalanges include the fingertips and these are associated with the mind; the second phalanges are the middle sections of the fingers and these are associated with putting ideas into action; the third phalanges are the lower ones and they are concerned with physical needs.*

Fingertips

These vary in shape and every shape tells its own story, as you will discover.

FINGERTIPS

ROUNDED	POINTED	SQUARE	SPATULATE
Hates tension and arguments	*Quick mind*	*Orderly*	*Active, could be sporty, actor, outdoor type*
Sociable	*Dogmatic attitude*	*Practical*	*Mind and body work well together*
Likes variety	*Few friends but is loyal*	*Statistical ability*	*Good scientist, lawyer, performer*
	Good organizer		
	If very pointed, a dreamer		
	Fussy about his image		

ROUNDED POINTED SQUARE SPATULATE

Side view of the fingertips

Look at the fingertips sideways on and you will see that they can be rounded, flat, bulgy and heavy or that they can be quite delicate but with a slight droplet at the apex.

COARSE   TAPERED   DROPLET

Coarse fingertips belong to those who are down to earth, materialistic, sometimes lazy, sensual and self-indulgent. Tapered fingertips mean a good mind and a spiritual outlook but the subject lacks strength and stamina. Droplets endow the fingertips with amazing sensitivity and the hands with dexterity. These people are clever with their hands and they rarely drop or break crockery. A droplet on Apollo together with a sloping head line belongs to a subject who has creative talent.

Fingerprints

The skin ridge patterns on the fingertips are the same fingerprints that the police use. These are formed in the womb and, unlike the lines on the hands, they never change. The most common patterns are the loop, the whorl, the arch and the peacock's eye. There are many composites and variations on these themes. (See page 92 for information on skin ridge patterns on the palm.)

FINGERPRINTS

LOOP	ARCH	PEACOCK'S EYE	WHORL	DOUBLE LOOP/WHORL	TENTED ARCH
Friendly	*Tense*	*Creative*	*Powerful personality*	*Indecisive*	*Shy*
Adaptable	*Introvert*	*May be artist, craftsman, writer, teacher*	*Self-centred*	*May be psychic if on Jupiter or thumb*	*Tense*
Team worker	*Shy*		*Success comes easily*	*Can stand outside of self*	*Obsessive (look at relevant finger to discover nature of obsession)*
Doesn't like commitment	*Worrier*		*Hard worker*		*Set views*
	Insecure		*Independent*		
	If arch comes to a point, obsessive		*Opinionated*		

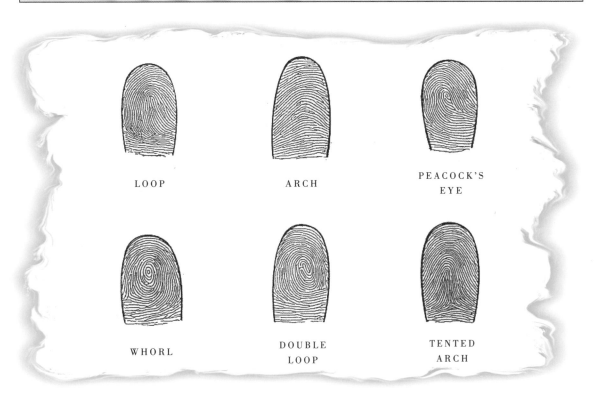

LOOP   ARCH   PEACOCK'S EYE

WHORL   DOUBLE LOOP   TENTED ARCH

Fingernails

The most interesting aspect to the nails is the way they show the current state of health of a subject. (This is covered in detail on pages 126–8.) Fingernails take about six to eight months to grow out. A sudden shock, an emotional upset

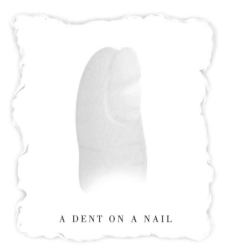

A DENT ON A NAIL

or spell of illness can be easily dated. This is because the body draws its energy inwards at such times and leaves little for the extremities. Therefore, the nails and hair either don't grow very much or grow weakly for a while. In this section, however, we will confine ourselves to personality on the nails.

Small nails are often found on a quick-minded, tense person who is tough on himself and others. Large nails belong on a slower type who may be a good crafts-man. People with large, long nails can be extremely cutting and hurtful. Curved nails suggest a need for security and, sometimes, greed and miserliness. Fan-shaped nails denote ambition.

NAIL SHAPES

ROUND	NARROW	SQUARE	SPATULATE
Friendly	*Tense*	*Scientific or mathematical mind*	*Active*
Adaptable	*Babyish*		*Scientific*
If wide, lacking in vitality	*Charming*	*Short, wide nails, witty and amusing*	*Ambitious*
	Demanding	*Volatile*	*Sporty*

THUMB	
A STRONG THUMB	*Hard worker, vigorous, extrovert, good powers of recovery*
A WEAK THUMB	*Unhealthy, dislikes challenges*
TUCKED-IN THUMB	*Insecure, anxious, tense*
LONG, THIN THUMB	*Philosopher, dreamer, may not do much work*
LONG, FAT THUMB	*Very strong-willed*
SHORT, THIN THUMB	*Passive, submissive*
SHORT, STUBBY THUMB	*Aggressive, tyrannical*
HIGH-SET THUMB	*Emotions are kept under control. Hard to fathom*
LOW-SET THUMB	*Could have hot temper. Open personality*
STIFF/FLEXIBLE THUMB	*If stiff, obstinate. If flexible, adaptable*

Thumb

The thumb should be about the same length as the Mercury finger. It is on the radial side of the hand, which represents the outward-looking, energetic and powerful aspect of a subject's personality. The thumb reveals the driving force that motivates us.

Here are several final points to consider. If the thumb turns back at the

HIGH-SET THUMB   LOW-SET THUMB

tip, the subject may be a spendthrift – for example, he may go out to buy one item and come back with something completely different. If the tip of the thumb is square, the subject is practical; if rounded, he springs to the defence of those who are weaker than himself; if it is spatulate, he is a craftsman, and if the thumb is not too thick in addition to being spatulate, he may be creative as well.

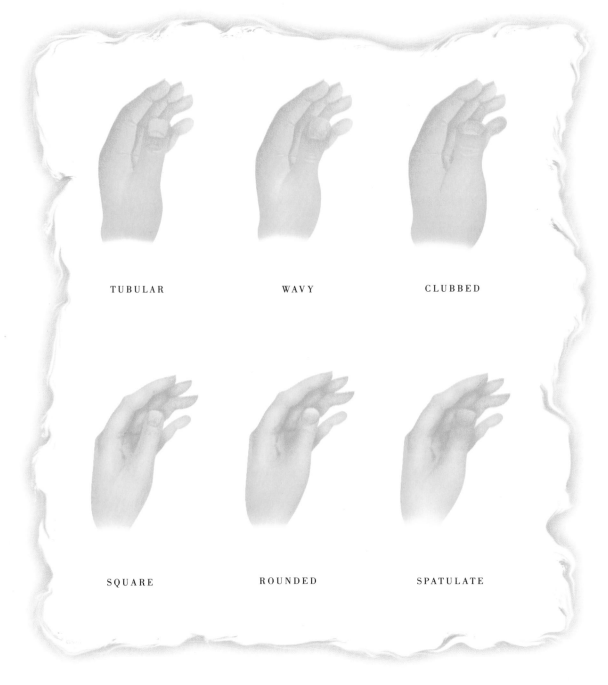

TUBULAR   WAVY   CLUBBED

SQUARE   ROUNDED   SPATULATE

The angles

If the knuckle at the angle of dexterity is prominent, the subject is well-organized. She may be a sportsperson or a practical worker. She likes doing things that have a kind of rhythm to them, such as playing tennis or grooming a pet.

DEXTERITY

HARMONY

ANGLES OF DEXTERITY AND HARMONY

If this angle is well defined, she enjoys creating a comfortable home and has good taste. She may collect lovely things and probably likes buying herself quality clothes. The greater the length between the two angles, the warmer the personality will be.

THE TOP PHALANGE

WEDGE-SHAPED   *Keeps going until he gets what he wants. Good lawyer or negotiator*

ROUNDED   *Relates well to others. Can exert authority when necessary*

FLAT   *Refined, gentle but lacks energy. Can get what he wants by nagging*

SPOKE-SHAVED   *Refined, pleasant, needs approval. Gives way to others*

WEDGE-SHAPED   ROUNDED   FLAT   SPOKE-SHAVED

The second phalange

If this is thick and straight, the subject sees things in black and white terms.

If it is cinched in or "waisted", he is more flexible in attitude.

THUMB PRINTS				
LOOP	**ARCH**	**PEACOCK'S EYE**	**WHORL**	**DOUBLE LOOP**
A team worker	*Shy*	*Very rare; shows creativity*	*Ambitious*	*Double-sided person*
Adaptable	*Repressed*		*Selfish*	*Tries to please everyone*
Reasonable			*Independent*	

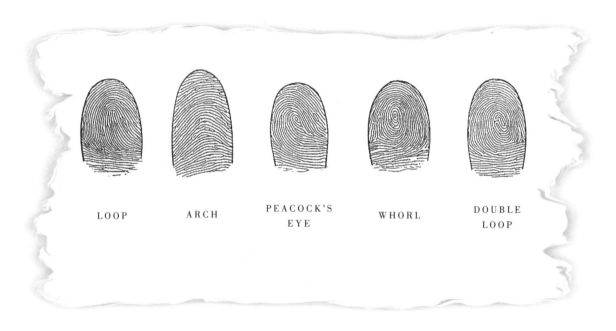

LOOP   ARCH   PEACOCK'S EYE   WHORL   DOUBLE LOOP

The mouse

Being the back of the mount of Venus, this indicates health, strength and vitality. The pressure inside the mouse varies according to the state of health and the state of mind. If it is firm at the time of the reading, the subject is fit and happy with himself. If it is weak and flabby, the subject may be ill or depressed.

MOUSE

TIMING ON THE HAND

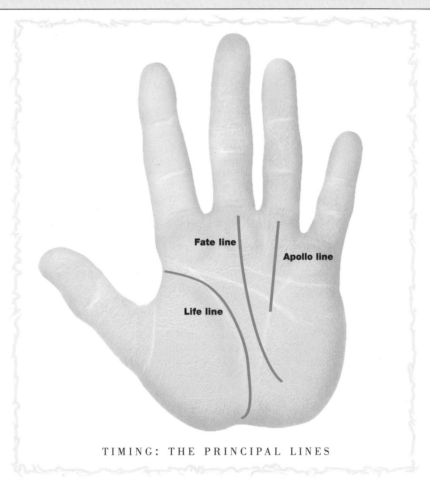

Fate line

Apollo line

Life line

TIMING: THE PRINCIPAL LINES

On the life line

Events can be timed downwards from the top of the life line but they can also be estimated upwards in conjunction with the fate line. Look at childhood and the early teens from the top of the life line downwards. Early life is happy if the lines are clear, difficult if they are disturbed. The loss of someone whom the youngster cares about is shown by a small line that drops down from the life line at this point.

For experiences from the late teens onwards, examine the lower part of the life line and the adjacent fate line. Look at the lines that radiate out from the mount of Venus and meet the fate line, because these will show times of stress and activity. By far the most important source of information on the predictive aspects of palmistry are found on and around the fate line.

TIMING AND THE JOURNEY OF LIFE ON THE HAND

Start at the bottom of the hand and follow the journey of life upwards, looking at a variety of lines as you go. Any line that merges with the fate line suggests an important new influence coming into the subject's life. Islands and disturbances denote confusion and hardship. If the lines are clear, the path of life is clear at the appropriate age. Check the various ranges given against the illustration shown opposite.

18/20 years Lines that touch the life line or the fate line or are on the mount of Neptune show the links to the outside world.

20/25 years A fate line distant from the life line here shows independence; the greater the distance the greater the degree of independence.

23/25 years If the fate line starts out close to Pluto, the subject will work away from home. An island on the inside of the lower part of the life line shows that the subject didn't get on with his parents in his early twenties.

25/30 years If the fate line leaves the life line at this point, the subject is trying to become independent.

30/40 years Decision lines that cross the fate line and "Y" formations on the fate line signal change. The subject may have to work hard at a relationship or cope with a job change. Any movement towards Apollo here could indicate a change to a more creative or appealing kind of job or maybe a move to a new home.

30/32 years If there are many lines gathering around the fate line, the subject will go through a restless period. Islands here denote financial shortages or stress.

40/42 years A broken fate line means a change of job. If the line dies away, there will be uncertainty. If the line stays clean, clear and single, the subject's life and career won't change. Two lines close together in a woman's hand mean work and children.

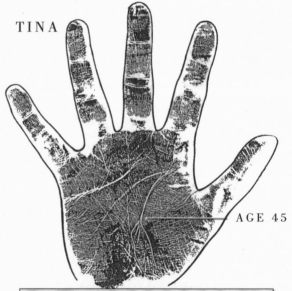

TINA

AGE 45

Tina's life line shows a change of circumstances at about the age of 45. She will move house, she may change her job or be faced with a change in her family situation. Good events are as likely to bring these changes about as bad ones.

42/55 years *If you find a series of fine lines adjacent to the fate line at this point, a reassessment of the subject's lifestyle is in the offing.*

55/60 years *By this time the Apollo line should be present and both this and the fate line will show how the subject's energies are being used. If the fate line doubles, the subject will become freelance or self-employed. If the Apollo line doubles, there will be a busy home life with children still around the home. Alternatively, the subject may look after someone else who is at home. If the fate line and Apollo line begin to close together, the subject will be going through a period of consolidation and ensuring an easy ride during the rest of his life.*

Old Age *If there are many fine lines at the top of the hand, the subject will overdo things and run out of energy. If there is a strong line running from the Apollo area to the Mercury finger, the subject will retire to be near his friends. Two short lines between the Saturn and Apollo fingers mean that he could retire close to his children. Lines extending up into these fingers suggest that the subject will be energetic and cantankerous in old age.*

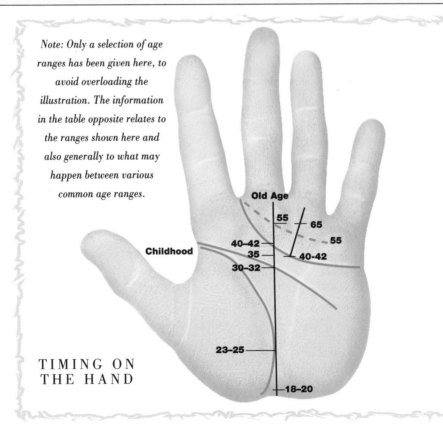

Note: Only a selection of age ranges has been given here, to avoid overloading the illustration. The information in the table opposite relates to the ranges shown here and also generally to what may happen between various common age ranges.

TIMING ON
THE HAND

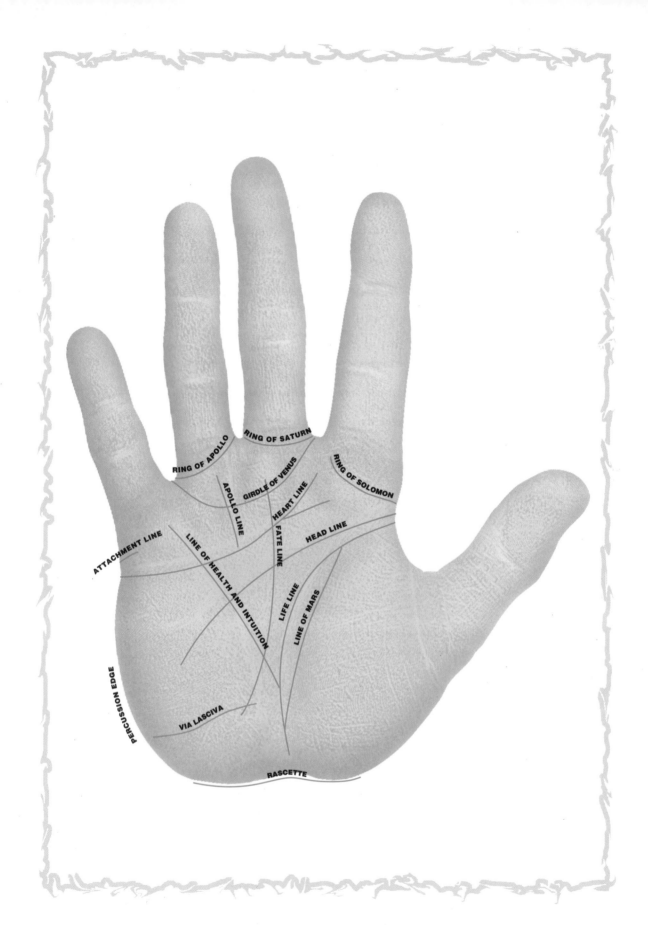

THE MAJOR LINES

*S*kin ridge patterns such as fingerprints remain the same throughout life, but all the lines on the hand, including the major ones, frequently change. A youngster's hand may not have many lines on it relative to an adult's. It is life's experiences that cause the lines to develop and give up our secrets.

Bear in mind that the major hand shows how we adapt to the world we live in, while the minor hand shows the inner feelings and traumas. The life line shows the general tone of the subject's life, her state of health (particularly at the time of the reading) and the major events of her life. It has a lot to do with where she lives and the sacrifices she makes for others – or otherwise. It should be healthy looking and of a deeper colour than

THE LIFE LINE

the surrounding hand.

The life line begins on or beneath the mount of Jupiter. If it curves around Venus, home and family life will be important and successful. If it floats away across the hand, career, travel or adventure may be more appealing to the subject than home and family life. If there is a fork, the subject will want, and probably get, both home life and an interesting lifestyle outside the home. If the line curves fatly around the mount of Venus, the subject has a terrific zest for life and plenty of physical energy and vitality. She is a home-loving, sociable, optimistic and fairly adventurous type. If the line is straighter, the subject is

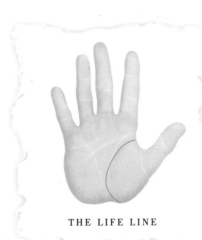

THE LIFE LINE

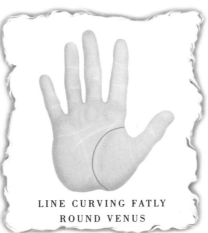

LINE CURVING FATLY
ROUND VENUS

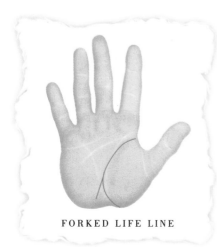

FORKED LIFE LINE

STRAIGHTER LIFE LINE

cool, detached and far more intellectual than physical in nature. Both types may or may not be sexy but they would approach this in different ways, with the fatter Venus being more lusty and the finer one being more clinical and clever in bed.

The starting point

Islands, feathering and general untidiness at the start of the life line denote a difficult start in life. Feathering right at the start of the line can indicate a mystery surrounding the subject's origins. A gap between the life and head lines with no other lines connecting the two is said to indicate independence and a reckless, imprudent nature. If the Jupiter finger is long and the Saturn short, this may be so. With a shorter Jupiter and a longer Saturn, the subject will be more cautious and home-loving but he will live the way he wants, without making much effort to suit others. Separate life and head lines may also be seen on those who stay single relatively late in life; the person who makes a family of his own early is likely to have tied life and head lines.

A life line that clings to the head line is supposed to denote a subject who takes a long

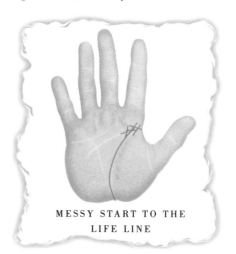

MESSY START TO THE
LIFE LINE

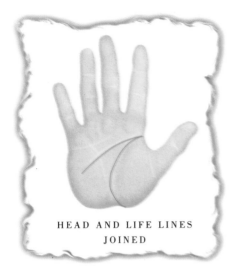

HEAD AND LIFE LINES
JOINED

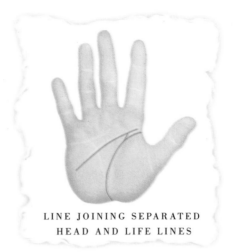

LINE JOINING SEPARATED
HEAD AND LIFE LINES

time to leave home or to separate from his family. This is often true, but there are cases which don't fit this pattern. For example, although the subject may leave home and set out on his own quite early in life, he remains close to his parents and background. He also has a cautious and controlled attitude to life and doesn't take chances very freely.

If the lines are parted but joined by criss-cross lines, there is evidence of difficulty in childhood. A single strong line suggests that the subject may have been partially or wholly brought up by someone other than his parents. A cat's cradle effect shows either that the subject hated school or that he liked school and saw it as an escape route because he was unhappy at home. Islands at the point where the head and life line part can indicate childhood

ISLANDS WITH LINE
DROPPING FROM THEM

CAT'S CRADLE

illness or emotional trauma. If a line drops down from the life line, the subject will have experienced some type of loss or disorientation in childhood.

The central area

Any interference in the line here shows an event. A family situation is shown by lines radiating out across the life line from Venus. A health or emotional setback could be shown by an island, a small break (with or without an overlapping join), a bar or some other kind of blockage. Minor

LONG ISLAND ON LIFE LINE

domestic problems can be seen by slight disturbances on the line, while major changes in lifestyle are indicated by major disturbances. A long island shows that the subject will do without something or make sacrifices for a while. He may take a course as a mature student, living on very little money, or perhaps support a partner.

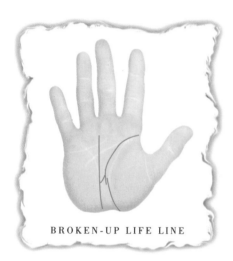

BROKEN-UP LIFE LINE

A common phenomenon these days is a line that ends prematurely in this area and is taken over by a heavy fate line. Another is of the life line breaking up and secondary lines appearing either side of where it should be. Such disturbances are caused by major shifts in lifestyle, often involving domestic upheavals and changes in location. Divorce and remarriage are classic causes of this kind of change in destiny.

Pits or dots on the life line suggest spinal trouble of some kind; you will find more about this on page 129. Any line that rises from the life line shows that

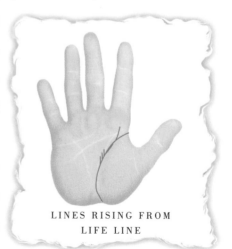

LINES RISING FROM
LIFE LINE

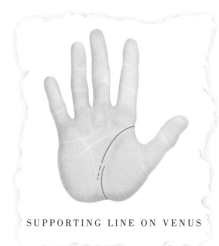

SUPPORTING LINE ON VENUS

the subject has improved his circumstances or will make great strides to do so at some future date. In some subjects you may find an island followed by such an upward branch. This may be read as a time of fruitful effort after a difficult or confusing patch.

The finishing point

A weak, flimsy or tasselled end to the life line suggests a long period of illness or incapacity later in life. However, lines can and do change, so even this depressing scenario doesn't have to happen. If the life line breaks up a bit towards the end but is supported by a strong new line on Venus, the subject may lose his home or family for a while, only to settle down happily again with a new set-up later.

If there is a very narrow fork with the two lines running more or less parallel, the subject will struggle to keep the home and family without help from others. An interesting career or a life spent travelling are shown by a life line that moves away from

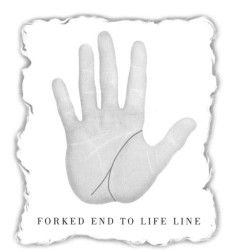

FORKED END TO LIFE LINE

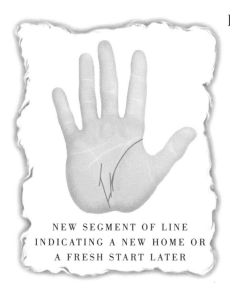

NEW SEGMENT OF LINE
INDICATING A NEW HOME OR
A FRESH START LATER

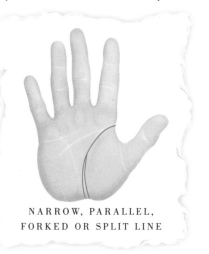

NARROW, PARALLEL,
FORKED OR SPLIT LINE

Venus and wanders out across the palm. The chances are that this subject will end up living overseas – he certainly won't remain in the area where he grew up.

PALM 🖐 WATCH

◁ *A short life line or a very broken one does not indicate serious illness or early death. It is most likely to indicate a major change of lifestyle. The minor hand will carry evidence of this when the cause is emotional and the major hand when practicalities are involved. Signs of this type of disturbance will usually be found on both hands.*

◁ *Sasha once came across a woman with no life line on the major hand. The subject said that she had been in a terrible car accident as a child and had almost died. She had recovered from this traumatic early experience and gone on to live a perfectly ordinary life.*

THE HEAD LINE

This line offers information about the way a subject thinks, her attitude to work and the kind of work she is likely to do. Disturbances on the line can indicate the state of her mental and physical health, especially concerning the head area. Features on this line may also reveal where she stands career-wise.

The starting point

Early difficulties in life are shown by islands, jagged formations, branches and crossing lines towards the beginning of the line. An exceptionally timid person will have a very tied head line which gives the appearance of not wanting to part from the life line at all. Alternatively, this may be

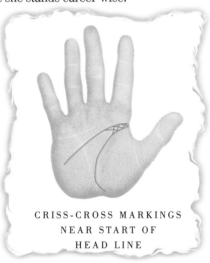

CRISS-CROSS MARKINGS
NEAR START OF
HEAD LINE

indicated by a line that starts within the life line. A more outgoing type of person has a line that separates fairly quickly from the life line or that is not joined to it at all. (See the section on the life line for other interpretations of tied or separated head and life lines.)

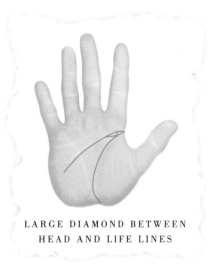

LARGE DIAMOND BETWEEN
HEAD AND LIFE LINES

Criss-cross marks at the start of the head line can indicate an unhappy family situation in childhood, especially if this affected schooling. If the subject hated school this would also show up as disturbances here. A period in the armed services shows up as a diamond that joins the head and life line at this point. Unless this large diamond is disturbed, he probably enjoyed this experience thoroughly. (Check to see if there is a full lower Mars for love of organized groups).

Central section

Jagged triangular formations that hang down from the head line, either near the start or further along the line, suggest periods of restriction and boredom. Both of us have seen these marks on people who have served time in prison. More rounded formations or islands suggest unhappiness or boredom at work.

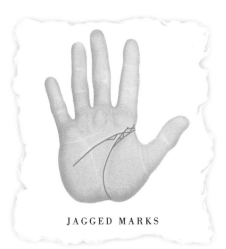

JAGGED MARKS

Any upward branch denotes a time of improvement through a new job, a profitable business venture, exams being passed or any other form of success. Falling branches don't really indicate losses but rather projects that are abandoned for one reason or another. A series of bunchy islands below the head line denotes headaches, often migraine. An isolated island, a break, a bar or some other

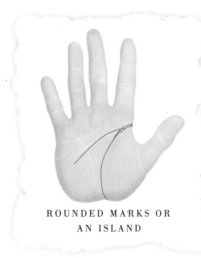

ROUNDED MARKS OR
AN ISLAND

RISING AND FALLING
BRANCHES

disturbance suggests a problem in connection with the head. If this is under the Saturn or Apollo finger it may indicate ear or eye problems respectively.

A clear, strong line suggests good mental faculties throughout life. A wavy line denotes mental or emotional problems that upset the subject's ability to think clearly. A straightforward career path is also indicated by a plain head line, while one that has many chops and changes will be shown by a wavy, disturbed line with some branches that rise and fall.

The tail end of the line

A long head line belongs to someone who has a good mind and uses it throughout life. Such a person is always interested in learning and in

LONG ISLANDS

keeping up with what is going on around him and is likely to be street-wise. This person will probably work all his life because he is a team person and enjoys the companionship of colleagues and also the feeling of being useful.

A short head line can belong to someone who switches off and gives up using his head early on but it can also suggest a specialist who knows a great deal about one specific subject. This person can either be extremely

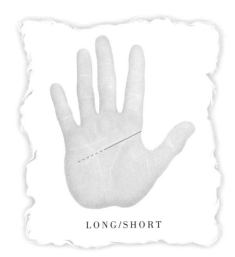

LONG/SHORT

successful or totally uninterested in work. If the former, he is likely to be in charge of others rather than a team member.

A straight head line is supposed to confer mathematical ability, while a sloping one belongs to a more creative, artistic or literary person. This does not quite compute but we have discovered that people who spend their entire lives working in an ordinary business environment, such as a shop or an office, have straighter head lines. The subject with a curved line may also live and work in an ordinary way but will have dreams, hobbies and interests of a creative kind. Curvy-line subjects are likely to work

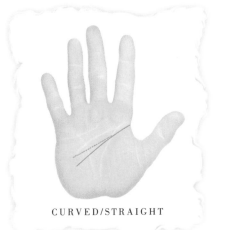

CURVED/STRAIGHT

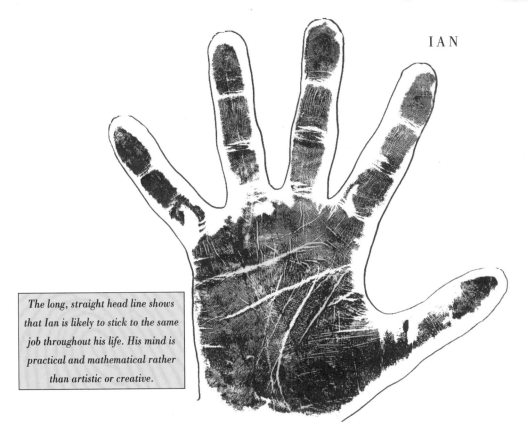

IAN

The long, straight head line shows that Ian is likely to stick to the same job throughout his life. His mind is practical and mathematical rather than artistic or creative.

PALM ✋ WATCH

◁ *A very deeply sloping head line suggests a subject who is so bound up with her own interests that she lacks a sense of proportion. A woman who fills her home with stray cats and dogs, for example, would have such a line – and probably fingerprints revealing tented arch formations here and there.*

◁ *Suicidal tendencies are said to be indicated by a steeply sloping head line. Certainly, a person with this type of head line is likely to be at the mercy of his emotions. If you know someone like this, encourage him to channel his unhappiness into a creative activity.*

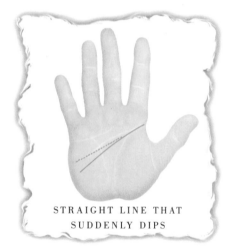

STRAIGHT LINE THAT
SUDDENLY DIPS

with people, while straight-line subjects prefer to work with figures and practicalities.

A straight head line that suddenly dips down the hand belongs to a subject who bottles up his temper and then explodes. If the area of upper Mars and the ball of the thumb are thick, this explosion is likely to be violent.

A shallow slope belongs to a balanced person who has a good mind and a good imagination, while a deeper one signifies a person whose imagination can override their common sense. A deeper slope that ends on Luna means that the subject has an active imagination which he may use in his work. Such a person is creative and probably artistic, musical or poetic.

Branches

Upward branches are always an optimistic sign

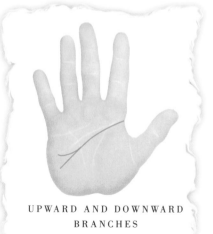

UPWARD AND DOWNWARD
BRANCHES

because they suggest times of improvement in the subject's mental outlook and her success ratio. A long upward branch indicates a change of direction that works out very successfully.

Doubled lines, forks and splits

A double head line where two lines are distinctly separate is a rarity. The few people we have come across with such a feature are more than a bit crazy. They simply cannot concentrate enough on anything to get anywhere in life and they end up mentally ill. Deep splits can indicate an inability to organize oneself, but they can also denote a subject who has different sides to his life – for instance, a business-man who is passionate about breeding dogs or ball-room dancing in his spare time.

Look at any forks that form at the end of the line and estimate where they are heading. For example, a branch towards Luna

DOUBLED LINES, DEEP SPLITS

endows even a practical person with imagination and creative talent, and also shows a liking for working with people. A branch to Mars or Mercury indicates courage and business acumen; to Apollo, family, social and artistic success.

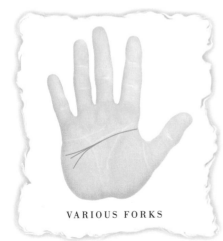

VARIOUS FORKS

Generally speaking, forks and splits bring versatility and a many-sided personality who has a variety of friends, interests and things going on in her life. She is probably very busy, and more than likely self-employed in at least one of her jobs. This subject is easily bored and needs plenty of variety in her life. She may also be unfaithful or inconstant in relationships, probably because she needs the challenge and the mental stimulation of many different types of people in her life.

Chained head lines suggest feeble-mindedness. Lines that fall apart to end in tassels suggest some failure of the head. This may mean increasing mental breakdown, Alzheimer's disease or something connected with the head, such as blindness or deafness.

HEART LINE

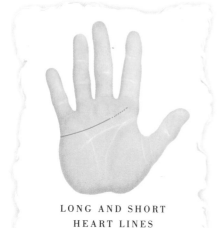

LONG AND SHORT
HEART LINES

THE HEART LINE

The heart line runs across the hand under the fingers and it refers to the emotions and the love life. Some health problems involving the chest cavity area are also indicated here.

There is some disagreement among palmists as to which end of the heart line is the beginning and which is the end. We use the more popular method of starting it at the percussion edge under the mount of Mercury.

Types of heart line

A long heart line can end on the mount of Jupiter or under the Jupiter finger. A short one ends under Saturn. A long heart line denotes an ability to give and receive love. A short heart line indicates a

AN ISLAND

blockage in the love and sex life. If the line is unblemished, the subject's romantic progress through life should be straightforward. A break in the line denotes breakups in relationships and probably a broken heart. Shallow heart lines that are closer to the fingers seem to show more of these breaks and disturbances than the deeper kind of line.

An island on the line can indicate a health problem, especially if it is directly under the mount of Mercury. If the island is elsewhere, this suggests a period of confusion and loss. If the island is large and isolated, the person will be subjected to some kind of shock, perhaps a partner walking out unexpectedly or maybe the sudden death of a partner.

Doubled heart lines denote great loyalty and sensitivity. Heart lines that are only partially formed or that disappear downwards into the head line suggest an unusual approach to love. This could also denote a problem with the love life.

DOUBLED HEART LINE

PALM 🖐 WATCH

◁ *A large gap between the heart and head line is supposed to confer tolerance and broadmindedness while a narrow one is supposed to denote a less tolerant attitude. If the gap is large because the heart line is high up on the hand, the tolerance will have more to do with an uncaring attitude than true broadmindedness. If the heart line is average but the head line is low and curving, the tolerance and broadmindedness are genuine.*

The heart line and health

A flaky area at the start of the heart line, under the Mercury finger, can be a warning of impending heart trouble. You must check the fingernails to see if they are blue or mauve in order to confirm this.

If the heart line dips when you push the subject's fingers back this can be an indication that the lungs and heart are not working properly. Once again, check the fingers: they should be a healthy pink colour, not bluish. The fingernails should be properly attached to the fingertips and not lifting away from them.

Any disturbance along the heart line where it begins to curve upwards towards the fingers can be an indication of breast problems. (And don't forget that men have "breasts", too.)

The fascinating information that the heart line carries about emotions, love, sex and relationships is to be found in the chapters on relationships, pages 102–20. (For additional information about the heart line and health, see page 129.)

LUNA | VENUS

FATE LINE

THE FATE LINE

If you learn nothing else in palmistry, try to grasp the meaning of the fate and Apollo lines because these really tell you what is going on in the subject's life like nothing else on a hand can. The fate line runs upwards from the bottom of the hand to the top.

Types of fate line

You will sometimes find a hand that has no fate line at all. In this case look at both hands carefully and see if there are some vestiges of a fate line. Any

TINA

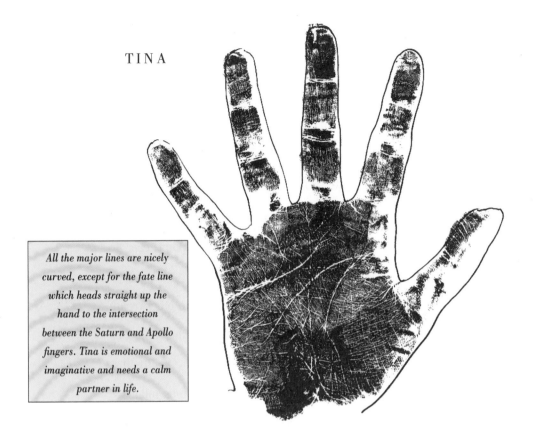

All the major lines are nicely curved, except for the fate line which heads straight up the hand to the intersection between the Saturn and Apollo fingers. Tina is emotional and imaginative and needs a calm partner in life.

bit of line will give you some information to go on. The line may be clean and clear, right up the hand from bottom to top, or it may begin halfway up the hand or nearer to the top. There may be fragmented segments of fate line, and these can be entirely independent of other lines or forced into the life line or some other line. This line may be vertical, diagonal or in pieces. When the life line is very broken or disturbed, the fate line often doubles up as part of the life line.

A long, straight fate line is quite unusual. This can be seen on the hand of a dutiful person who follows the fate that seems to be set out for him and invariably does what is expected. If the line begins to break up towards the top of the hand, the subject may tire of his mundane existence and begin to question what he is getting out of life. If the fate line veers towards Jupiter and ends up at the top of the hand, he will take whatever comes his way and turn it to his advantage. A broken fate line seems to suggest someone who is prepared to set his own agenda in life. Fate lines often vary quite a bit between the left and the right hands. The fate line on the left hand will tell you what a subject wants from life, while that on the right hand will show how the reality of his existence differs from his desires.

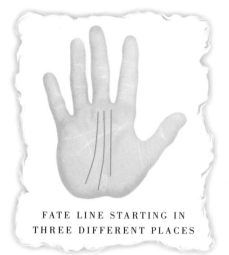

FATE LINE STARTING IN
THREE DIFFERENT PLACES

The starting point

Assuming that the fate line does start at the lower end of the hand, this starting point can be anywhere from inside the life line to well over on the mount of Luna. The proximity or otherwise of the fate line to the life line shows the subject as being close to or detached from the family. If it begins inside the life line, the subject's family will have a strong influence on his early life. This influence may be very helpful, by giving him a happy childhood and a good education and also by helping him develop a healthy level of self-esteem. He may start out in the family business, only branching out on his own when the fate line detaches itself from this area of the hand. The other side of this coin is that the subject's early life could be full of restrictions as a result of family pressure to conform to religious or social standards. This kind of family may not be interested in the subject's real needs, only their view of how he should live.

Material concerns such as money, business and possessions may dominate the subject's early thinking, possibly as a result of his upbringing, and may well colour his attitude throughout life. Consequently, he may remain very materialistic, or later in life he may discover different values and reject this early training. A beginner could not be expected to work out these permutations just by looking at a subject's hand, so if you see this kind of formation, ask what happened and build up your fund of knowledge.

If the line begins on Luna, outsiders could be instrumental in helping the subject find his way in life. However, this is not necessarily so, because self-motivation could also apply. Another possibility is that the subject is able to use his imaginative and creative powers to achieve success or that travel or foreigners could figure in his destiny.

If the line begins anywhere else on the lower part of the hand, the subject is independent and self-motivated. Other events that kick-start his life will be shown by lines that join, leave or interfere with the fate line at this point. The most likely arrangement denoting a difficult start is a fate line that begins on Neptune and is irregular, islanded or disturbed in its early stages.

Early struggles, or otherwise

Take a ruler or pencil and place it across the hand from the knuckle that joins the thumb to the hand. Everything below this refers to the time up to the early or mid-twenties.

Obviously, if there is no fate line in this lower area of the hand, there may be nothing special to report upon in the subject's early life. In such cases it is as well to look at the beginning parts of the life and head lines because information may be stored there instead.

Lines that run into the start of the fate line suggest that the subject was physically and mentally ready for a permanent rela-tionship at a young age and that probably he married or lived with someone very early on. Whether this turned out to be a life-long relation-ship or an early experiment that didn't stand the test of time can be seen by the situation further up the fate line. If lines enter from the Venus side of the hand, the subject will have settled down with

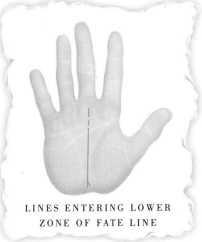

LINES ENTERING LOWER
ZONE OF FATE LINE

someone from his own locality who may have been known to his family. If the line enters from Luna, the partner will be a stranger. If the subject married early but there are no lines entering the fate line, there is an element of convenience in the arrangement and one can only hope that love comes along later.

Islands, bars, breaks and influence lines that drift across this area of the fate line show early difficulties. An island suggests a period of confusion, loss and unhappiness, while a bar represents a bar to the subject's progress. Breaks and gaps are a common sight on the fate line and can indicate setbacks, but they also denote times when the subject chooses to change direction. If there is an overlap the subject won't have suffered too much from the change in circumstances, and he will probably make the new start before he has finished tying up the loose ends of the old situation.

STRAY INFLUENCE LINE
CROSSING THE FATE LINE
FOLLOWED BY A JAGGED
DISTURBANCE ON THE LINE

If the fate line seems to jump towards the thumb side, the subject takes steps to improve his status out in the world (especially if this is on the major hand). If it jumps towards Luna, he is more interested in family life, hobbies and other personal matters (be sure to check the minor hand as well as the major one here).

A fine, stray influence line running across the fate line, especially if there is an island or some other disturbance following it, hints at a problem within the subject's family during his childhood or teenage years. Check the early stages of the life line for confirmation.

The middle area

A fate line beginning in the middle of the hand, on the plain of Mars, shows that the subject doesn't really find his way in life until around or after his

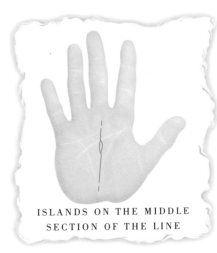

ISLANDS ON THE MIDDLE
SECTION OF THE LINE

mid-twenties. The same pointers we have already explored in connection with the other major lines apply here, too. So, for example, a line that joins the fate line in this area can indicate a romantic relationship or simply a person of influence entering the person's life at this point. If the joining line coincides with a split on the fate line, there are decisions to be made. If the joining line is itself split, the subject will have to work at the relationship.

Islands suggest shortage of funds and breaks, bars or other disturbances show times of difficulty. If the line jumps towards the thumb side of the hand, the subject will find a goal to aim for and will achieve some worldly success. A leap towards the percussion side denotes a subject who is currently more interested in personal and family matters. If the fate line, or some part of it, is joined at any point by a parallel line running closely alongside it, a period of self-employment could be on the cards. On a woman's hand, it can indicate children and a

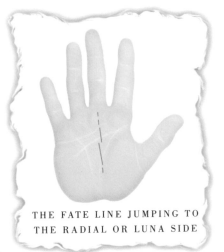

THE FATE LINE JUMPING TO
THE RADIAL OR LUNA SIDE

career proceeding in tandem. The underlying theme is that life becomes very full and busy.

Joining lines or influence lines here can indicate the birth of a child and the beginnings of a family. Lines that leave the fate line and wander over to the life line denote that the subject returns to her family or her roots for some reason. A likely scenario would be if a marriage broke down and the subject went back to her parents for a while.

A DEEP JOINING LINE AND
ALSO AN INFLUENCE LINE
RUNNING ACROSS THE
FATE LINE

If the fate line ends in a fork at this point and then starts again a little higher up, the subject will abruptly end a situation and take another path in life; for example, by leaving a job or changing career.

Timing

Palmists disagree about the timing of events on the hands, and it is our opinion that you can't be precise about this. For example, many palmists consider that the fate line crosses the head line at about the age of 35, whereas we think this is closer to 30. However, head lines vary, so it is best to be a little vague. If you see an event, describe it to your subject, give her an age band in which you consider it likely and then ask her to give you the exact dates. See the section "Timing on the Hand", pages 53–5.

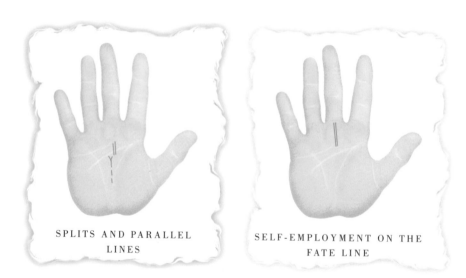

SPLITS AND PARALLEL
LINES

SELF-EMPLOYMENT ON THE
FATE LINE

PALM 🖐 WATCH

If the fate line disappears, the subject's life will change. Life may become easier, or it may be that she discovers what suits her and this knowledge means that she is not driven to make further adjustments in her life. In short, she ceases to strive.

The rest of the fate line

The fate line crosses the heart line at some point from the subject's late thirties to mid-forties, depending on the depth of the heart line. If the line breaks around this area and forms a collection of smaller parallel lines, the subject may well become self-employed. Alternatively, her working life may become extremely varied and interesting. (All the comments about islands, forks, influence lines and so on that we have covered in the earlier sections apply equally to this area of the fate line.)

FATE LINE TAKING OVER
FROM THE HEART LINE

The fate line often breaks up at this point with other lines running parallel or around it. Sometimes lines join the fate line from around the junction of the life and head lines; sometimes they enter from somewhere beneath the Apollo mount. Extra lines can show additional sources of income.

You will now have to watch to see what direction the line (or lines) takes in these final stages. If the line (or lines) travels towards Jupiter the subject

---

PALM 🖐 WATCH

◁ *Lines joining the fate line here can indicate new relationships and happier times late in life after, for example, divorce or loss. Lines leaving it can indicate departure from a job, a marriage or any other unsatisfactory situation.*

◁ *A doubled fate line may signify a double life (check the head line for two jobs and the attachment lines for double relationships). It can also mean that the subject dislikes what he is doing and would rather be where he thinks the grass is greener.*

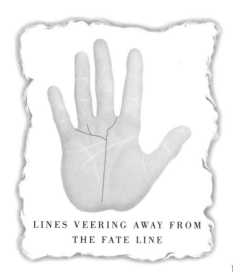

LINES VEERING AWAY FROM
THE FATE LINE

will put her efforts into making a success of her career. If, as is often the case, the heart line is taken over by this section of the fate line, she will put her emotional energies into her job rather than her personal life. Either way, she should end her life feeling that she has achieved something.

If the fate line (or lines) ends on the Saturn mount, the subject will work hard throughout his life. He may do this because he needs the money or he may just be the kind of person who likes to keep himself busy. He could become rich as a result of his efforts, but the quality of his life may be sacrificed in the process.

If a line or branch veers off in the direction of the Apollo finger, the person will end his days happily pottering around with his friends and family. He may not be rich but he will be happy and balanced in his outlook. If the fate line disappears altogether in this upper region, he may lose his money or cease bothering to strive.

If a line joins the fate line (or reaches across to the Apollo line) at this stage, the subject will inherit money, property or something else of material value. A line that wanders over to Apollo can also indicate an additional property, maybe some place reserved for weekend breaks or holidays. (Always check to see if the family line is doubled, because this is a good indication of an additional property being in the offing).

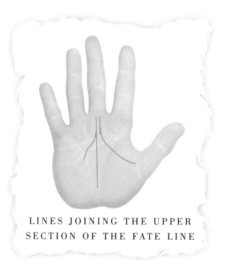

LINES JOINING THE UPPER
SECTION OF THE FATE LINE

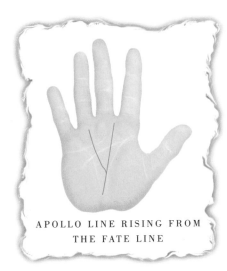

APOLLO LINE RISING FROM
THE FATE LINE

THE APOLLO LINE

The Apollo line is also known as the Sun line by many palmists. In astrology, the Sun is ruled by Apollo, the Roman god who is associated with success, music, art, love-making, creativity and children. It follows the same direction as the fate line but heads up towards the Apollo finger rather than Saturn or Jupiter. There are many hands with no Apollo line at all and most only have a partial one beginning somewhere under the head line.

If there is no Apollo line, the subject may never be really interested in

HELEN

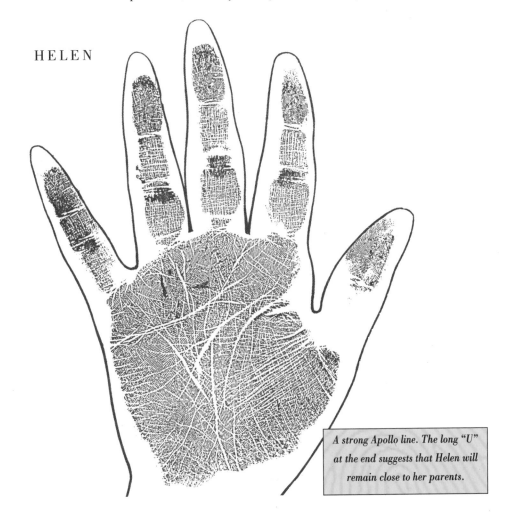

A strong Apollo line. The long "U" at the end suggests that Helen will remain close to her parents.

making a home for himself or a family. If there is a clear line, the home will be established early in life. If the Apollo line jumps towards the percussion side of the hand, home life will become important at the age at which the jump occurs. Any line (or lines) that links the fate and Apollo lines indicates some form of work from or very close to the home. Such lines also indicate a need for self-expression in the subject's working life. Self-

DOUBLED LINE (APOLLO LINE PLUS COMPANION)

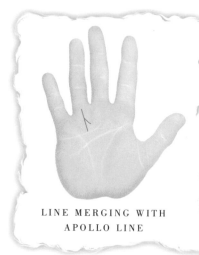

LINE MERGING WITH APOLLO LINE

expression is even more important when the Apollo line begins as part of the fate line. In such a case, fame, fortune or a highly obvious form of success is a strong possibility.

The upper area

Take a close look at the lines on the mount of Apollo, between the heart line and the Apollo finger – there is a wealth of information stored here.

An Apollo line or a collection of small lines in this area is pleasing to find because it indicates happiness in later life. It also denotes a comfortable and loving home life to be enjoyed in old age. A doubled line denotes living alongside a partner but not really participating in each other's lives to any great extent. Such subjects and their partners have separate interests. If the Apollo line disappears at this point, the subject should be warned not to risk his home on a speculative venture.

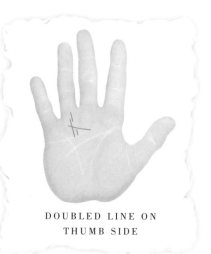

DOUBLED LINE ON THUMB SIDE

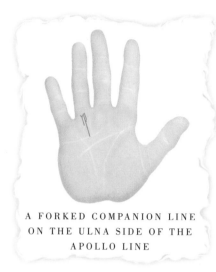

A FORKED COMPANION LINE
ON THE ULNA SIDE OF THE
APOLLO LINE

The thumb or radial side of the Apollo line

Companion lines that are close to the Apollo line on the thumb side of the main line mean a wish to move house that will probably not be fulfilled. If there is a connecting line between the main line and the subsidiary ones, the move should take place. Lines that merge into the Apollo line denote new people coming into the subject's life. This can actually be an indication of a late marriage or other home-based partnership. Other small lines on the thumb side of the Apollo line suggest an interest in creative hobbies, the arts, counselling, healing or any other form of work from home. In this case, the work is a pleasure as well as a means of earning some useful money.

The percussion or ulna side of the Apollo line

Lines that reach towards Mercury suggest an active mind that needs like-minded people around for mental stimulation. Small lines and especially a small fork formation here show that the subject will take care of his parents to some extent later in life. With "Y" formations of any kind, there is love and care poured into the needs of others. This may be a sick partner, sick parents, pets who need attention or long-term disabled children.

Lines that run parallel to Apollo but not absolutely adjacent to it suggest love at a distance. This could indicate concern for family members, an ex-partner or a close friend living far away.

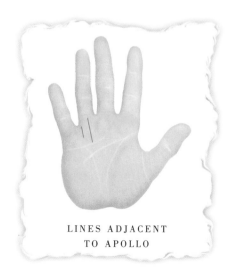

LINES ADJACENT
TO APOLLO

THE MINOR LINES

The major lines, as we have seen in the preceding chapter, are the life line, the head line, the heart line, the fate line and the Apollo line. All other lines are called minor lines. Very few people have all the various minor lines present on their hands, but most of us have a few. We'll look at them in alphabetical order, beginning with a group of the most common lines.

The attachment lines

These are small but often deeply scored horizontal lines that run across the percussion and on to the mount of Mercury, in the area between the Mercury finger and the heart line. It is highly appropriate that these lines should appear here because the mount of Mercury is concerned with communication and the heart line is associated with the feelings.

In the past, palmists stated that one attachment line meant that the subject would have one marriage, while two meant two marriages. Nowadays we think that the number of lines evident at any given time indicate what the subject wants and may or may not represent what will actually happen. That said, the old wisdom has proved its validity many times. The only certainty is that these lines can alter dramatically when the subject has a change of heart or lifestyle.

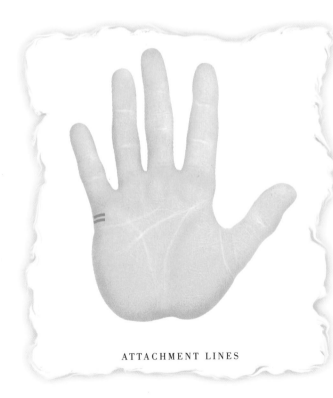

ATTACHMENT LINES

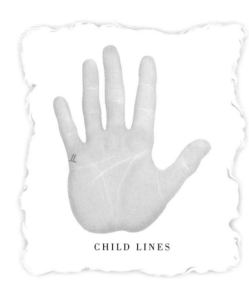

CHILD LINES

Child lines

These travel vertically down through the attachment lines. They must pass through one or more of these lines to be significant. We suggest that you use a magnifying glass and also that you roll the percussion side of the hand between your fingers and study the formations that you see there very carefully. Always check this kind of information on both hands because the minor hand will probably carry a more accurate account.

The girdle of Venus

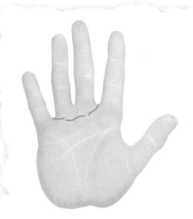

GIRDLE OF VENUS

There may be a whole girdle or parts of one – usually one or both of the two ends are present and the middle section is missing. The girdle may be evident on one or both of the hands, and it may be scored very finely or quite deeply. It denotes sensitivity of a kind that allows the subject to sympathize with others and also to be vulnerable and open to hurt himself.

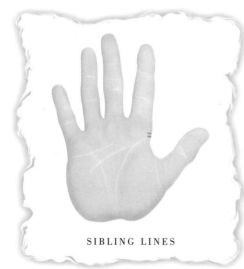

SIBLING LINES

Sibling lines

These lines echo the attachment lines but on the other side of the hand. They are usually more lightly scored than the attachment lines.

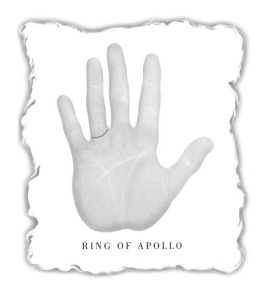

RING OF APOLLO

LESSER MINOR LINES

You can also expect to find some of the following minor lines.

Ring of Apollo

This may suggest a temporary blockage to happiness in a relationship or disappointment in some hobby or creative interest.

Company lines

Fine lines that reach up between the Apollo and Saturn fingers show that the subject will never be alone for long and she should end her days with someone to love.

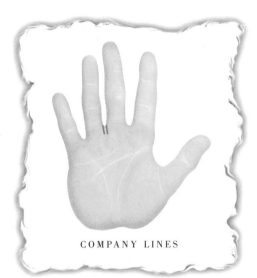

COMPANY LINES

Family ring

This can be clean and clear but is more often flaky or chained. The clearer the line, the more straightforward home and family life is likely to be. If there are many moves of house or chopping and changing within the family the line will be disturbed. Sometimes there are extra bits of line to one side or the other. This suggests additional homes or maybe time spent sorting out a parent's property. Dots, breaks and discolorations here denote problems with the family or the parents.

FAMILY RING

Lines that radiate out from the family ring denote family interference. It is worth tracing their course to see precisely in which area or areas of the subject's life this interference is making itself felt. A strong crease extending outwards from the family ring indicates closeness to the parents when it turns upwards towards the top of the palm and closeness to the partner and children when it turns downwards.

Health line or via hepatica

The Ancients thought the health line offered information about the state of a person's liver, hence the name via hepatica. Nowadays it is

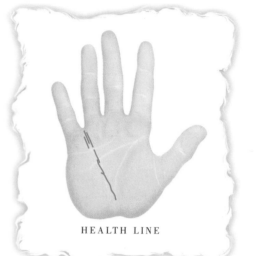

HEALTH LINE

believed to reveal more about our spiritual pathway through life than our liver. The health line can be part of the line of intuition or a separate entity entirely. It usually zooms straight up the hand from the Luna/Neptune area to the mount of Mercury, although in some people it may be found running into and forming part of the healing striata. Sometimes there are two such lines running parallel, in which case palmists tend to refer to the inner one as the health line and the outer one as the line of Mercury. If you are confused by all of this, don't worry. Any line in this area will give you information on health and healing.

The existence of a health line denotes that the subject is likely to be health-conscious, with a desire to look after himself and also others. If the line is feathery, he will be keen to take care of family members or others who are close to him. If

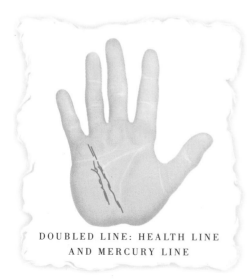

DOUBLED LINE: HEALTH LINE
AND MERCURY LINE

it turns around and ends up on an attachment line, there will be a very important relationship that will have so great an impact on the subject that his health will be affected for a while.

Healing striata

This distinctive mark is found on the mount of Mercury. It comprises three vertical or slightly diagonal lines, sometimes crossed by a fourth line. These lines indicate an interest in medical work or healing of some kind, including spiritual healing.

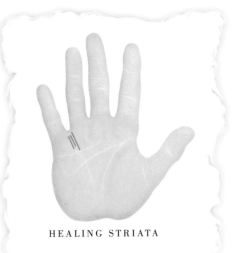

HEALING STRIATA

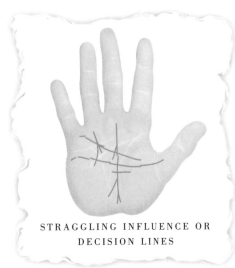

STRAGGLING INFLUENCE OR
DECISION LINES

Influence lines

Sometimes referred to as decision lines, these are stray fine lines that wander across the major lines. They show a change of mind, often as a result of outside influence. If the lines come from within the mount of Venus, parental figures or other older members of the subject's family will either be the cause of the change or will be implicated in it. If they come from the percussion side of the hand, outsiders are involved.

Curve of intuition

This line denotes strong powers of intuition. This intuition is not simply a case of deduction, intel-

CURVE OF INTUITION

ligence and/or a natural grasp of psychology, but also something that has a true psychic source. More about this can be found on pages 121–4.

Line of Mars

This line sits inside the life line and it may be as strong as or stronger than the life line itself. It provides protection from danger, loss, illness and other misfortunes and it is an excellent backup

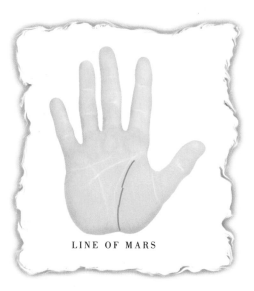

LINE OF MARS

in cases where the life line itself is weak.

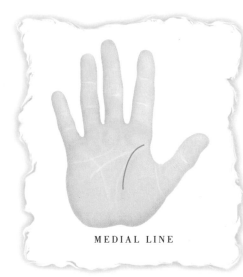

MEDIAL LINE

Medial line

If you confuse this with the line of Mars, don't worry – just ask your subject a few questions and you will soon discover which it is. This often starts as part of the life line and then peels off from it on the Venus side of the line. The line of Mars, if present, will lie between the medial line and the life line. The medial line is fascinating because it indicates that the subject has abandoned something (or someone) which didn't work out the way he wanted and has made a fresh start.

Ring of Saturn

A person with this mark is a loner or a non-relater of some kind. He may have a depressed and melancholy nature or he may bury himself

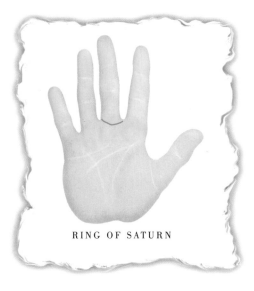

RING OF SATURN

in some form of scientific research, ignoring or losing out on normal human relationships.

Ring of Solomon

This denotes wisdom, counselling ability and sympathy for the plight of others. Psychologists, carers and medical practitioners should have such a line. If the heart line touches or crosses this line, the subject will make his career in a caring profession and may even substitute this for real family life.

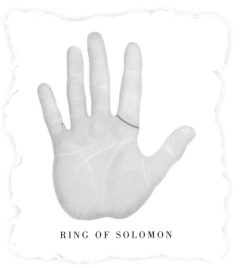

RING OF SOLOMON

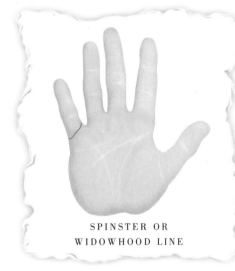

SPINSTER OR
WIDOWHOOD LINE

Spinster line

This used to be the symbol for a spinster. It is also called the widowhood line and can indicate the loss of a partner through death or some other event. The subject will spend a substantial part of his life alone. We have also discovered this on the hands of those who feel alone or lonely even within an existing relationship.

Spiritual growth

Fine lines between the Mercury and Apollo fingers denote spiritual awareness and growth.

Teaching aid

A line that reaches to the inside of the Mercury finger signifies teaching ability. If this touches the health line or healing striata, it suggests an

SPIRITUAL GROWTH

TEACHING LINE

interest in teaching health and hygiene. A square on Jupiter is another indication of teaching ability. A girdle of Venus also suggests an urge to learn and to teach.

Travel lines

These are found on the percussion from the heart line downwards. See pages 153–5 for more details.

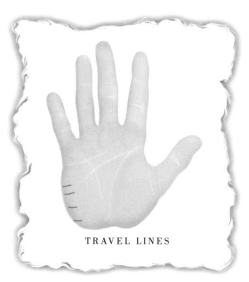

TRAVEL LINES

Trident

A trident on the mount of Apollo shows that the subject will always land on her feet financially.

Via lasciva

This used to be called the poison or allergy line. If the line is clear, there is sensitivity to drugs and the subject is probably better off turning to natural remedies or homeopathy.

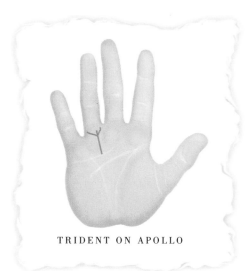

TRIDENT ON APOLLO

VIA LASCIVA

MARKS, LOOPS AND WARTS

*T*his area of palmistry can drive a beginner to distraction. You may won-

der if such and such a mark is a cross, square, grille or whatever, or if

it is perhaps simply a stray joining of two other lines. Try not to worry about

this and just bear in mind that if something in a hand strikes you as odd, you

should look it up and check on its possible meaning. Many of these marks come

and go with events in life. Some are lucky, some less so. Some types indicate

protection, while others denote a restriction in some area of life. The most

common types of marks are listed in the following tables and shown in the

accompanying illustrations.

MARKS	WHAT THEY MEAN	WHAT THEY LOOK LIKE
Cross-unlucky	On head or life line: shock, operation, illness.	
	On heart line: emotional shock.	
	On Apollo line: property problems.	
	On Saturn mount: money worries.	
	On Luna mount: sea sickness.	
Cross-lucky	On Jupiter: teaching ability.	
	On Apollo: a windfall, royalties, commission.	
	On Mercury: competence with computers etc.	

MARKS	WHAT THEY MEAN	WHAT THEY LOOK LIKE
Square-unlucky	Restriction. On head line, work problems. On heart line, emotional restriction. On life line, could be protection or restriction.	
Square-lucky	Protection, from danger, harm, loss, depending upon which line it covers.	
Triangle	Talent. Look at placement. For example, may be a great sailor if on Luna.	
Star-unlucky	Supposed to be a truly malevolent sign. If the star is red, there will be a severe problem. See the location on the hand to work out the problem.	
Star-lucky	On the mount of Jupiter: wealth through achievement. If on this mount and close to the heart line: the subject will marry money. On Apollo: fame and fortune.	
Grilles	These may not be easy to spot but if you see one, it always indicates illness or trouble in the appropriate area.	

DISTURBANCES ON THE LINES	WHAT THEY MEAN	WHAT THEY LOOK LIKE
Tassels	Usually at the end of a line: illness, weakness, senility.	
Dots or pits	Illness. These come and go.	
Chains	Confusion, lack of self-esteem. A troubled patch to live through.	
Islands	Always important. Trouble, shock, loss, sacrifice, hardship, unhappiness. If long, a refusal to face reality. If short, a short sharp shock.	
Discoloration	Blotchy, discoloured patches or shiny, red, mottled patches denote illness.	
Branches	Upward branches on lines denote improving circumstances, downward ones denote giving something up. Falling branches on the heart line denote a flirt.	

Skin ridge patterns

Many hands carry the occasional loop or whorl marking. Loops are more common and whorls only appear on the mount of Mercury or around the boundary between upper Mars and Luna. (See also the chapter on Fingers for loop and whorl markings on the fingertips, pages 46–7.)

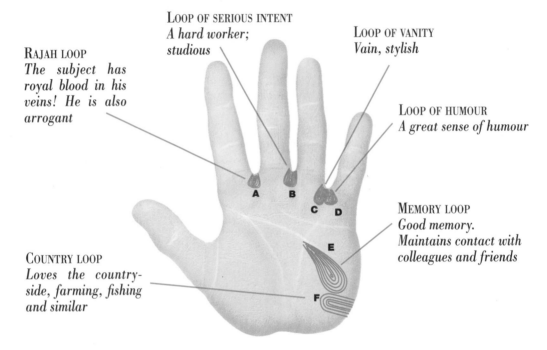

LOOP OF SERIOUS INTENT
A hard worker; studious

LOOP OF VANITY
Vain, stylish

RAJAH LOOP
The subject has royal blood in his veins! He is also arrogant

LOOP OF HUMOUR
A great sense of humour

MEMORY LOOP
Good memory. Maintains contact with colleagues and friends

COUNTRY LOOP
Loves the country-side, farming, fishing and similar

Warts

Warts on the palmar side of the hand suggest that the subject may be her own worst enemy; if they are on the back of the hand, someone else is giving her problems. Children's warts are meaningless. If a wart appears on the Jupiter finger or mount, the subject's self-confidence is being undermined; if on or around Saturn, basic necessities may be a worry; if on Apollo the problems will be connected with the home, family or a desire for self-expression; if on Mercury, a deliberate misunderstanding is involved. A wart on the thumb indicates a major barrier to the subject exercising her willpower. If it is on the first phalange of any finger, the problem will bring mental anguish; if on any other phalange, there will be practical problems.

HAND GESTURES

*I*nfants will point to something that attracts their attention long before they are able to articulate their interest. Similarly, in adulthood we can make a hundred different gestures while talking. The way we use our hands is involuntary and unconscious, and it says a great deal about us as individuals. The lines and marks that travel up the hands are an extension of the meridian lines of energy and emotion that make each one of us what we are.

The movements that reveal

Watch carefully when people are debating a point on television. If they massage the top phalange of their fingers, they are considering what they are going to say. If they massage the top of their thumbs, they are wondering if they have the will and determination to speak out. On news programmes, the camera will sometimes home in on a person who is massaging the logic areas of their thumbs. This shows that they are under stress and struggling to cope with the situation they are in.

You may also sometimes notice someone with beads of perspiration that look like strings of pearls on the fingertips. This person is going through some form of mental anguish. Observe the way people place their fingers when they sit down at a table. If the Saturn and Apollo fingers hug each other, the subject is longing for security and understanding. This person could be going through a stressful time, possibly even the breakup of an important relationship. He is in need of help.

If the Saturn finger overlaps the Apollo finger, the subject is

SATURN AND APOLLO FINGERS
HUGGING TOGETHER

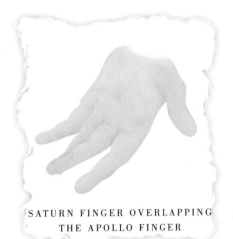

SATURN FINGER OVERLAPPING
THE APOLLO FINGER

trying to protect himself from hurt by projecting the day-to-day mundane matters that he can cope with and hiding the emotions that he can't control. If the Apollo finger overlaps the Saturn finger, the subject wants to be noticed and to project himself out on to the world.

If a finger starts to bend inwards, watch to see which finger it is and how much it is bending. A slight bend means slight apprehension and cautiousness. This subject has been hurt and doesn't want to be hurt any more, but she is prepared to go forward and continue living her life. If the finger is curled right in, she feels desperate, hopeless and unable to cope with the emotions that are raging inside her.

FINGER BENDING

If the Mercury finger falls away from the other fingers, the subject wants to be independent and to do things her own way. If the hand is relaxed when placed on the table and the Mercury finger is well away from the other fingers, the subject is in a restless frame of mind and is ready for a change.

MERCURY FINGER HELD
AWAY FROM APOLLO

Watch any conductor leading an orchestra: his fingers rise and fall as he feels how he wants the music to be played. Study a contestant on any serious quiz show: while being quizzed, she may have her Jupiter and Mercury fingers locked over the top of her Saturn and Apollo fingers. This is her way of saying that she wants to take control of the situation and to use her mind to its greatest capacity. When the quiz is finished, the fingers will go back to their normal position.

Talking with the hands

Open fingers denote an open mind, closed fingers a closed one. When a normally open-minded subject talks about details, she may also hold her fingers closely together.

Curved fingers are saying that the subject is unsure of what he is talking about. Straight fingers tell you that he is comfortable with his topic. If an expert on the television talks with his fingers straight and closed, he is saying that he doesn't want anybody doubting his authority or questioning his knowledge.

When you are watching someone talking authoritively, perhaps organizing others in some capacity, you may notice the Jupiter and Mercury fingers sticking straight out. They are communicating that the subject is the boss and should be listened to.

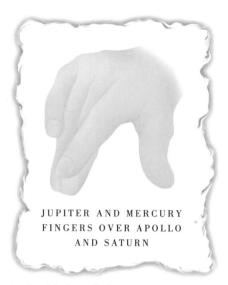

JUPITER AND MERCURY FINGERS OVER APOLLO AND SATURN

The fist

The fist has always been seen as a symbol of power and aggression. Normally the thumb is held outside the fist, showing that the subject is comfortable with his willpower and strength of character. He may be assertive, but this is under control. If it is held inside the fist, the negative traits are held inside. The subject could eventually explode in a fit of temper or aggression but he is more likely to be feeling deeply depressed. Either way, the will and strength of the person's character are being driven inside and kept in an emotional pressure cooker.

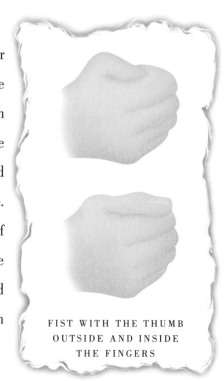

FIST WITH THE THUMB OUTSIDE AND INSIDE THE FINGERS

HOW TO TAKE HANDPRINTS

There are various ways of taking handprints. Malcolm obtains good results using a photocopier. A more traditional method, and one favoured by most professional palmists, involves using a tube of black water-soluble printing ink, a tile, paper and a hand roller. Don't worry if you don't get a clear, full print at your first attempt. Even professional palmists sometimes have to take several prints to obtain one that is usable. It is important to ensure that the palm is flat on the paper and that potential problem areas – the fingers and the centre of the palm – make full contact with the surface. The best way of achieving this is to ensure that the subject's hand is completely relaxed.

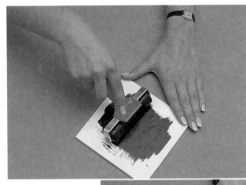

The steps

1. Take a few pieces of kitchen towel to make a soft base and then put a couple of sheets of ordinary typing or photocopying paper over the top.

2. Squeeze a little of the printing ink on to the tile. The ink is about the consistency of toothpaste and you will need about the same amount that you would use to clean your teeth.

3. Roll the roller back and forth through the ink, covering it well. If you find a roller difficult, try using a stencil foam pad (available from any good DIY store). The ink should be tacky and not wet.

4. Ask your subject to take off her watch or any precious rings and to roll up her sleeves, then pass the roller firmly over the palm, fingers and thumb.

5. Take her hand, which you should ask her to relax, and place it on the paper.

6. Press down fairly firmly (but not too hard) all over the hand and fingers, with extra pressure applied at the base of the fingers and the thumb.

7. Go round the hand with the felt-tipped pen. If

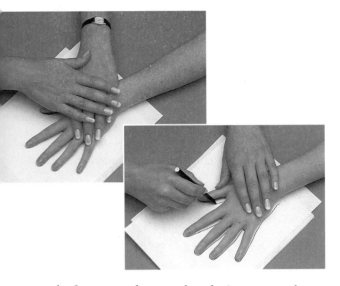

Quick & easy method

If you want to take the odd print without going to the trouble of using the full kit, the process can be simplified further.

Take a few pieces of kitchen towel to make a soft base and then put a couple of sheets of ordinary typing or photocopying paper over the top. Cover the palm of the hand with some dark-coloured lipstick, then press it down on the paper. If you are left with a gap in the middle of the hand, fold a few extra pieces of towel to increase the height at the base, cover this with a couple of sheets of paper and try again.

If you want a clear outline, draw around the hand with a felt-tipped pen before asking the subject to lift his hand off, wrist end first.

the fingers are close together, don't try to part them. 8. Ask your subject to lift her hand up from the wrist end while you hold the paper down. Repeat these steps for the other hand.

At the end of print-making, take your subject to the sink, fill it up with warm water and give her soap and a clean towel. Reassure her that any residual paint on her hands will come off later. The ink is water-based and any traces on clothing will come off in the wash.

Make a note on the bottom of the page of the subject's name, age and whether she is right- or left-handed.

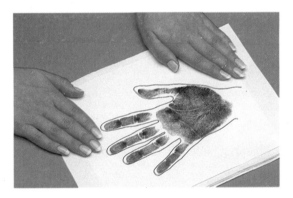

K I T   F O R   T A K I N G   P R I N T S

🖐 *A ceramic tile – the kind you would use for tiling a kitchen or bathroom.*

🖐 *An artist's paste-up roller.*

🖐 *A tube of Lino printing ink; any dark colour will do. This is a water-based product which washes off hands and clothes without doing any permanent damage.*

🖐 *A felt-tipped pen.*

HOW TO READ A HAND: THE BASICS

PART TWO

So far we have followed the traditional chapter sequence favoured by palmistry books since time immemorial, starting with hand shapes and ending with the smallest marks. Unless you have some experience in hand reading, you will probably feel weighed down by the amount of information. In short, you won't know how to apply the knowledge you have been given. All palmistry books, even this one, give too much information for a true beginner, so it is a good idea to confine yourself to the basics to begin with. Professional palmists can take in a great deal of information almost at a glance, but if you try to do the same and look at too much at once, you will only become confused. The aim of this chapter is to identify these basics and provide you with a blueprint for future hand readings.

Getting started

A sensible first step is to make sure that you read hands in a good light and with a magnifying glass nearby for smaller features. Learn to take prints, as these will bring small lines and marks into view. If you can't take a print, try smoothing some talcum powder or coloured face powder on the hands. Then follow the ten steps given below.

Ten steps to success

1. Look at the back of the hand first and assess its general shape.

2. Still looking at the back of the hand, check the relative lengths of the fingers and then see if any of the fingers lean towards their neighbours. Do the fingers spread easily or are they held closely together? At this point, you can also take in the general shape and appearance of the finger-tips and the nails. Don't forget the thumb.

3. Now, turn the hands over and take a look at the shape of the palm. Assess the thickness of the fingers and the fatness or otherwise of the phalanges. Do the same for the thumb. Check out the fingerprints for whorls.

4. Check the colour of the hands; you may wish to take another look at the backs of the hands at this point. Feel the hands to see if they are firm or flabby. Test the fingers for flexibility at the tips or where they join the palms. Test the thumb for flexibility. Flexible and floppy fingers denote a soft

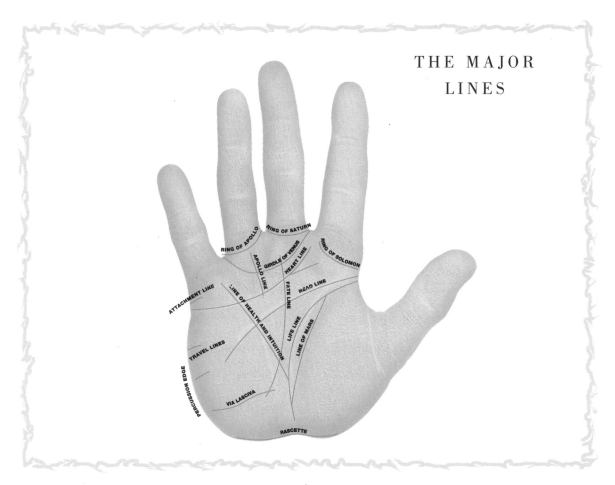

THE MAJOR LINES

Labels on the hand diagram: RING OF APOLLO, RING OF SATURN, RING OF SOLOMON, GIRDLE OF VENUS, HEART LINE, APOLLO LINE, ATTACHMENT LINES, LINE OF HEALTH AND INTUITION, FATE LINE, HEAD LINE, LIFE LINE, LINE OF MARS, TRAVEL LINES, PERCUSSION EDGE, VIA LASCIVA, RASCETTE

and malleable nature; firmer hands suggest a firmer nature as well as good health.

5. Check the "setting" of the fingers to see how they join the hand. Look at the thumb and see whether it is high or low set and how your subject holds it when the hand is relaxed.

6. Now begin to look at the mounts: are any of them prominent, large or particularly obvious in any way? Note any mounts that are cramped or insignificant.

7. Begin to analyse the lines, starting with the major lines in the following order. Look at the life line, then move to the head line and the heart line. Examine the fate line carefully because this will probably give you more information than almost anything else on a hand. Look at the Apollo line.

8. There are many minor lines, so check which ones are present and which are not. Read the minor lines. If you get lost here, go through the mounts of the hand one by one and see what appears or does not appear on each one. Look at them in this order: the mounts of Jupiter, Saturn, Apollo, Mercury, Venus, Luna, upper Mars, lower

Mars, Neptune, Pluto and the plain of Mars. Some lines will cross over a number of mounts, as in the case of a health line or a girdle of Venus.

9. Take note of any discolorations, warts or any other features that stand out and catch your eye. If there is a wart, assess its position and what it might mean (see the case study of Rita, below).

10. If your subject is interested in knowing about a particular aspect of his life, select those lines or areas of the hand that will give you the information. (We'll be looking at a selection of these aspects next in Part Two.) For example, if relationships are at the top of your subject's list, look at the heart line, the Venus area and the attachment lines. If it is a job that he is worried about, check the head line and the fate line and also such small features as the money-maker line. Check also the general hand shape and the fingers to see the kind of job at which he would excel.

RITA – A SEARCH FOR HAPPINESS AND PEACE OF MIND

Rita's hand is rounded, with strong lines – especially the fate line. On the face of it, life should be good for her, but this is not the case. Rita suffers from depression and is unhappy in her personal relationships. Why?

As you will see, Rita's is a convoluted case and unravelling the major events of her life would tax the professionalism of the best palmist. In cases like this it is sometimes necessary for the palmist to check with the subject that they are on the right track; a probing question or two usually does the trick. Professional palmists are supposed to be able to work out what the events are unaided, but it wouldn't hurt for you to ask your subject a few more direct questions.

Rita's hand provides a good illustration of how a focal point – in this case, a wart (d) – may encourage a palmist to look at many different areas of the hand in order to build a picture of a subject's life.

Rita's head line (a) is longer and stronger than her life line, which is broken and tasselled at the end (b). Influence or decision lines on Rita's life line show two changes, possibly occurring about five years apart (c and c).

The significance of the wart (d) is underlined by its position in relation to the lines radiating around it. One line joins the head and heart line and then dives into the mount of lower Mars (e). This denotes sexual problems related to childhood bullying or abuse. The fine lines that join the heart and head lines and cut through the fate line (f) suggest a marriage with little communication and no affection. The new Apollo line forming above the wart (g) suggests happiness later in life. Interestingly, it has transpired that Rita is moving out of the country to make a new life with a lady-love. Note the line that falls away at the end of the heart line and joins the start of the head and life lines (h). This often signifies a search for one's true sexual identity.

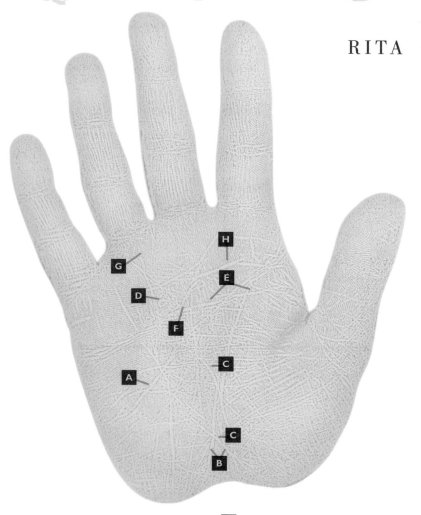

RITA

A Head line

B Life line with tasselled end

C Decision lines on the life line

D Wart

E Joined head and heart line descending into the mount of lower Mars

F Fine lines joining the heart and head line

G New Apollo line

H Line at the end of the heart line joining the start of the head and life lines

RELATING TO OTHERS

We shall be dealing with the potentially thorny topic of love relationships in two parts. Here, we look at what the lines, especially the heart line, reveal about us – the kind of people we are and how we relate to our nearest and dearest. In "Hand Signals for Lovers" (see pages 116–20) we explore what hand shapes can tell us about the sexual side of ourselves.

The Heart Line

A long, curved heart line shows the ability to give and receive love and affection. This subject chooses a partner on the basis of a need for affection, shared interests and a deep spiritual feeling of togetherness. He can be impulsive and sometimes disappointed and hurt by those he loves. If a relationship ends badly, he becomes very upset and pours his feelings out to his friends. After this, he gets over his hurt and goes on to love again – albeit with a little more caution.

A short, deeply curved heart line that reaches up to the gap between the Jupiter and Saturn fingers belongs to a demanding person who is sexually active and rather selfish about his needs. He can pour his energies into work at times and forget to relate to others at all at times.

A gently curving heart line with branches shows a sensible attitude to relationships. Friendships are not neglected, and partners are chosen partly from love and attraction and

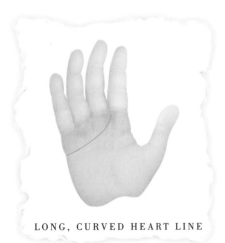

LONG, CURVED HEART LINE

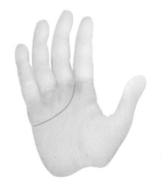

SHORT, CURVED HEART LINE

CURVED LINE WITH BRANCHES

partly for practical reasons. The deeper the heart line, the more passionate the feelings. The subject is passionate, caring and a good friend all at the same time.

A long, straight heart line belongs to someone who puts a great deal into relationships. This person helps the partner to achieve his or her ambitions and that partner will be chosen carefully, with due attention to status, background, education, shared interests and so on. This subject is a caring employer, a good friend and a reliable mate. He is not over-impulsive and he takes relationships seriously, but can

IAN

Ian has a straight heart line with a girdle of Venus showing slightly above it, indicating that he is serious about relationships and more sensitive than he appears to outsiders.

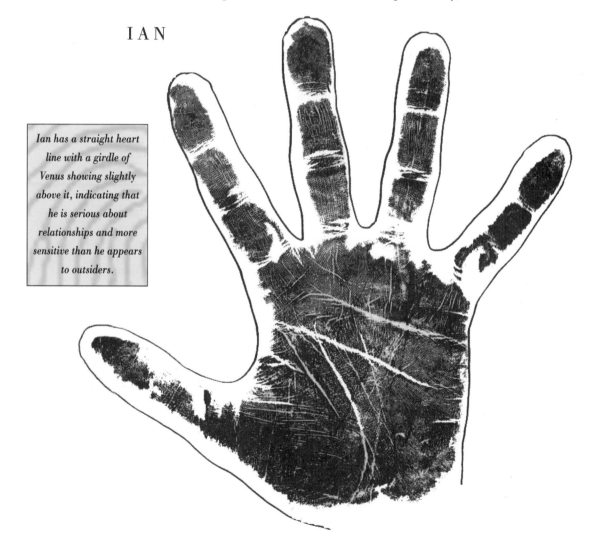

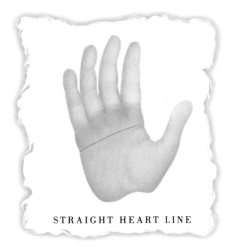

STRAIGHT HEART LINE

SETTING OF THE HEART LINE

be a bit withdrawn and cold at times and may seek to dominate the relationship. He is probably more interested in all-round compatibility than in sex.

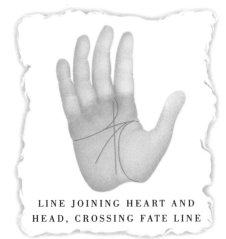

LINE JOINING HEART AND HEAD, CROSSING FATE LINE

If this subject is hurt, he says little, broods on what has happened and rarely regains the ability to trust or love unconditionally again.

A high-set heart line belongs to a calculating character who can distance himself from the troubles of others. A subject with a lower heart line loves to talk about love, sex and feelings and to relate to a partner. He is emotional and caring, and his heart tends to rule his head.

A line that joins the head and heart line and cuts through the fate line

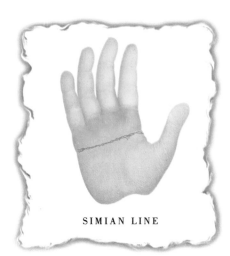

SIMIAN LINE

suggests at least one relationship in which there is a lack of real communication. This type may marry someone who never really communicates and whom he never really understands.

Sometimes there is no real heart line on the hand at all – the heart and head lines become one thick line called a simian line. A subject with a simian line is obsessive and explosive in

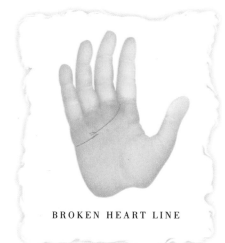

BROKEN HEART LINE

SEMI-SIMIAN LINE

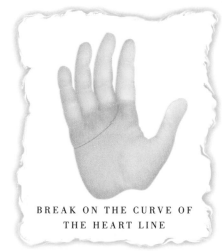

BREAK ON THE CURVE OF
THE HEART LINE

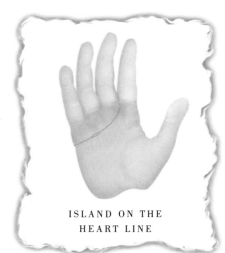

ISLAND ON THE
HEART LINE

nature. Semi-simian lines denote problems left over from childhood which may never be resolved. A broken heart line shows a broken heart. A heart line that has a small-break where it turns upwards suggests that the subject finds love, friendship, affection and sex but not all in the same place!

A large island on the heart line denotes a shock to the system from a broken relationship. In some cases, the partner disappears and even just "goes out for a packet of cigarettes and doesn't come back".

A double heart line denotes great sensitivity and loyalty on the part of the subject.

If the heart line dives downwards into the head and life line at its ending, there is something odd about the subject. He may have been abused as a child or he may be confused and unhappy about his sexual nature.

Don't forget to look at the mount of Venus to see if it is well developed, suggesting energy, affection, sexuality and a desire for the good things of life. Maybe it is cramped, suggesting a more mental approach or a cold heart.

FLAKY HEART LINE

A flaky heart line is quite common on young hands and it indicates a minor health problem, possibly a shortage of potassium.

Attachment lines

Victorian palmists called these marriage lines but the hand doesn't recognize marriage, so nowadays

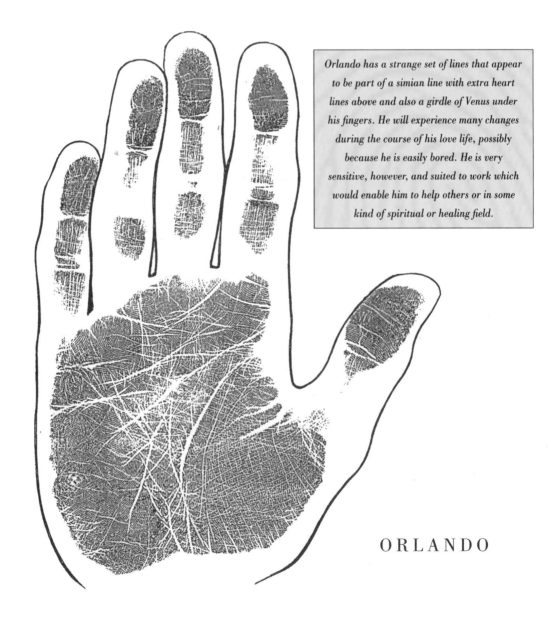

Orlando has a strange set of lines that appear to be part of a simian line with extra heart lines above and also a girdle of Venus under his fingers. He will experience many changes during the course of his love life, possibly because he is easily bored. He is very sensitive, however, and suited to work which would enable him to help others or in some kind of spiritual or healing field.

ORLANDO

ATTACHMENT LINES

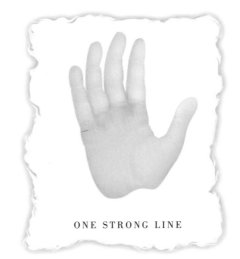

ONE STRONG LINE

we call them attachment lines instead. Fold your hand slightly and look between the crease at the bottom of the Mercury finger and the start of the heart line. If there is more than one line, read them upwards towards the finger.

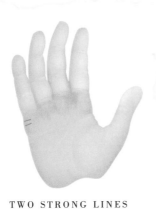

TWO STRONG LINES

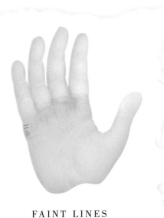

FAINT LINES

One strong attachment line signifies a person who wants to relate emotionally to her partner. She marries for love and tries to have a fulfilling life with her partner. If for some reason she finds herself single again, she may come across someone new to love and feel deeply about or she may never get over the loss of the loved one.

Two strong lines belong on the hands of people who like relationships. If a hand is full of fine lines and there is also a girdle of Venus present, the subject can over-react and become over-emotional, making marriage a tempestuous affair. If there are three lines, the subject tries to find his inner self through relationships instead of through himself.

Faint lines refer to early romances that have some meaning for the subject. A great many lines simply mean that the subject is not particularly interested in relationships at the time of the reading or that she is looking around in a fairly casual way. Some of these lines will eventually fade while others become stronger.

If a relationship is in the process of breaking up, the attachment line may have developed a deletion line through the end of it. It may become islanded, tasselled or broken up and it may even bleed for a while.

The end of the line

The ends of the attachment lines give the palmist some information on the progress of a relationship.

One clean, straight line shows a strong marriage that is kept together by mutual understanding and a realistic attitude to what can be expected from the partner. This type of line is found on earthy, square hands that are not covered by fine lines.

Two lines that run parallel and almost side by side show that the subject is simply coexisting with another person. He will put up with his partner's irritating ways and escape from them by being deeply involved in his own interests. The marriage drifts on but the couple avoid any meaningful contact with each other. If the lines are exceptionally fine, the subject may derive some comfort from the relationship but he may put his career first.

ATTACHMENT LINE
WITH UPWARD BRANCH

If the fate line melts into the heart line on the mount of Saturn, the subject will throw himself into work, neglecting his partner. He may avoid sex altogether or he may keep his sex life going with an affair outside marriage. In this case it is worth checking the fate line to see if any lines merge with it, indicating an important new relationship while the marriage still exists.

One straight line with an upward branch is a very common sight these days. There are two possible explanations for this kind of line. The first is that the subject forms a relationship with someone who does well in a career at some point during the partnership. The second is that the subject herself does well and that it puts a strain on the partnership. If the latter, this subject is self-sufficient and career-minded and has a tendency to ignore the emotional needs of a partner. A well-paid woman with such a line may look down on her partner, causing resentment on both sides. She may eventually prefer to be alone rather than to continue to "keep" her husband. Such a line, therefore, can be an indication of a relationship in trouble.

ATTACHMENT LINE
CURVING DOWN

When the line curves down, the subject will find the relationship disappointing. He may feel put upon, stifled or dominated by his partner. If the subject has a whorl on the Apollo finger, he may not want to make any effort to make the partnership work.

A line with an island on it means that the subject

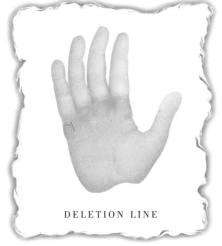

ATTACHMENT LINE WITH
ISLAND

will never get his life together in the way that he wants. Perhaps what he wants is impossible to find, or he may want different things from one day to the next. He may want to have a partner but then be unable or unwilling to go on and make a relationship work. The marriage can survive if the subject is fairly reasonable and if he is willing to forgive and forget past problems.

DELETION LINE

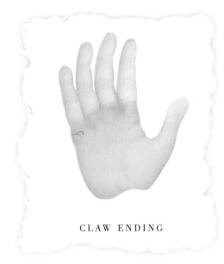

CLAW ENDING

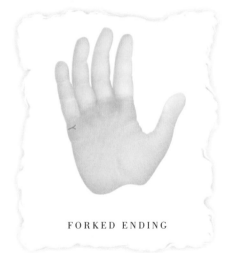

FORKED ENDING

Sometimes you will see a deletion or blocking line at the end of an attachment line. This is a temporary line that shows you that the subject is either in a relationship that is breaking up or that he has recently broken up from his partner.

A claw-like ending to the attachment line shows that the subject keeps on harping back to a past partnership and won't put it behind him. He may harbour feelings of hatred and spite against this previous partner and may try to influence his children against her.

A fork at the end of the line reveals a relationship in trouble but one that

PALM 🤚 WATCH

◢ Stars, redness or patches of discoloration on or near the attachment lines suggest a relationship in trouble.

◢ All the information given here, as elsewhere in the book, applies equally to heterosexuals and homosexuals. The hands of gay people are no different to those of straight people.

◢ A broken life line with the fate line or some other line continuing in its place suggests a major change in the subject's life, with a broken relationship a strong possibility as the cause.

◢ Lines that run into the fate line or the Apollo line often signify the start of important relationships. Refer to the chapter on timing to see when this is likely to be – see pages 53–5.

can be salvaged and the problems resolved if both partners work at it.

A line that forms a ring around the base of the Mercury finger is a "widow line" and indicates that the subject may be widowed. It doesn't always appear when the partner dies but is usually a reliable indicator. This line may also appear when a subject is married but still feels lonely.

Childhood legacies

When the head and life line are tied, the subject may have been over-protected in childhood. Religious or social pressures may have been brought to bear. The subject is cautious and naive. If the parents were domineering, and unwilling to give the subject affection in childhood, he may have grown up finding it difficult to love.

When a child has been brought up in a tense, violent atmosphere, he may only relate to love in a violent way. Women who have disturbances at the start of the life, head and fate lines may spend their lives wandering from one violent or otherwise unsatisfactory relationship to another. If there are only faint sibling lines or if they are completely absent, check whether your subject was an only child. Only children who were considered precious by their parents will want the same treatment from others later in life.

A Jupiter finger that is shorter than the Apollo finger denotes emotional caution and a damaged ego. The subject may or may not be highly sexed and she will keep her heart to herself. When this person eventually falls in love, she does so very deeply and passionately.

A subject whose head and life lines are sepa-rate will want to take the lead in a relationship and to be in control of the situation. People with this feature can be flirtatious, brazen, very attractive

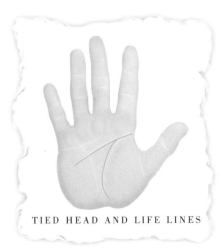

TIED HEAD AND LIFE LINES

and possibly shallow. They can become restless if things don't go according to plan. These people will have been encouraged to be independent in childhood and may have had to fend for themselves. If the gap between the head and life line is filled with jagged marks, childhood will have been a struggle and unhappy, possibly as a result of being institutionalized. Such children have to learn to love much later in life. Look for a rounded island where the head and life line part – a feature often found on the hands of those brought up in an institution or boarding school. If the end of the thumb is large and/or carries a whorl fingerprint, the subject will go after what he wants with unshakeable determination.

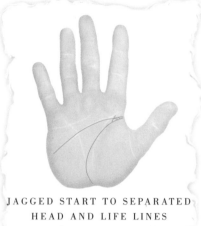

JAGGED START TO SEPARATED
HEAD AND LIFE LINES

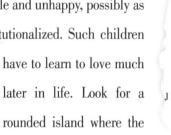

HEAD AND LIFE
LINES SEPARATE

GUIDE TO THE FINGERS

FINGER	HOW THE FINGER RELATES
SHORT JUPITER	*Self-conscious, lacks self-esteem. Falls deeply in love and can be hurt. If this finger bends, very sensitive and also very attached to the family*
LONG JUPITER	*Well-developed ego, career-minded, opinionated, selfish*
SHORT SATURN	*Impulsive, silly*
LONG SATURN	*Thoughtful, materialistic, workaholic, in love with money, science or religion*
SHORT APOLLO	*Little interest in home or family, recreation or creativity*
LONG APOLLO	*Sensitive, emotional, loving, sacrificial. Loves family, hobbies, friends. Creative*
SHORT MERCURY	*Shy, repressed, could have sexual problems*
LONG MERCURY	*Talkative, sensitive to others. Persuasive, sexy*
STRONG THUMB	*Strong sense of own needs, obtains own requirements*
WEAK THUMB	*Walks in the shadow of others, lazy, lacks willpower. May whine and complain*

FAMILIAL RELATIONSHIPS

*O*ur relationship with our parents can have major implications for our emotional growth and well-being, as we have already seen (pages 111–2). In this section we will look at the lines concerned specifically with how we relate to siblings (defined here as brothers and sisters) and children. When looking for signs that will shed light on relationships, remember that the minor hand will often provide a more accurate picture than the major one, so to be doubly sure in your assessment, read both hands.

Sibling lines

The so-called sibling lines are found at the edge of the hand under the Jupiter finger. These lines don't "read" in quite the same way as the attachment lines because the relationships in question are not normally as demanding or interdependent. Basically, if there is a strong line, there will be a strong attachment to a sibling; if there are two lines, two siblings will be important. The subject may actually have many brothers and sisters but not all of them will be close to him. If there are no lines, the subject probably didn't have any close relationships in childhood, and if he did those concerned have long since moved out of his life.

If the line bends up to the Jupiter finger, the relationship is still a good and close one. If it bends

SIBLING LINES

downwards, the relationship will still exist but it is not likely to be so successful. Perhaps this sibling was closer to the parents than his other "sibs". If the line is forked, broken, messy or otherwise disturbed, the sibling himself will be going through a difficult patch and the subject will be somewhat worried about him. If the line is broken, the sibling will have left or be leaving a job or a relationship. If there is a square over the line, the sibling is frustrated and restricted. In short, these lines show the condition of the sibling's life in miniature at the time of the reading.

Child lines

Look at the attachment lines through a magnifying glass in good light and you will see some fine lines running vertically down through them. These are child lines. They are not always easy to read because sometimes there can be a number of fine lines in this area. Look for the strongest of the lines. The number of lines should correspond to the number of children a subject has or will have; ie, one line equals one child, two lines equal two children and so on. Confusion can arise because lines may refer to children that the subject becomes associated with, possibly by forming a partnership with someone who already has children or merely by looking after them for other people.

You must also note carefully which attachment lines the child lines actually pass through. If there are two or

CHILD LINES

three attachment lines and the child lines pass through all of them, the subject will have children as a result of a first marriage or relationship. If these child lines only pass through the highest attachment line, the child or children will be associated with a subsequent relationship.

Child lines may not be in evidence even on adult hands. They tend to show up most clearly when children are an issue in the subject's life; for example, if he or she is interested in having them.

You may also like to consider the following items of palmist lore. Straight lines suggest boys while oblique ones suggest girls. A line with an island or other disturbance on it indicates that the child is either ill, unhappy or creating problems for the subject. A line that splits into two can indicate twins in the subject's family, either his own or a relative's.

A short line that ends in a squiggle can indicate a miscarriage. If, in addition, there are dots in evidence on the attachment lines, a termination could well be indicated. If the dots appear on a lower attachment line, the termination would be associated with an early relationship; if on the upper line, with a later one. Lines that don't touch any attachment line suggest a partner who refuses to have children.

HAND SIGNALS FOR LOVERS

What kind of partner do you want? You may not know the answer to this question, but your hand can probably give you a few helpful clues. Next time you meet someone new, look at their hands and see if they tell you something. If you find the person attractive, it may be that you share a similar hand type. Sometimes like attracts like.

A square-handed farmer, for example, is quite likely to choose a square-handed wife who could help him around the farm. Such people are reliable, warm-hearted, easy-going family people but their love lives can become routine and boring unless they are constantly fired with romantic ideas. Sexually, they like their pleasures and quickly become irritable if denied, but unless the head line slopes downwards they are not likely to be particularly clever or imaginative lovers.

Strong, rounded, conic hands are usually found on women – men's hands tend to be more chubby. Women with these hands enjoy flirting and being chatted up. Their male counterparts like to think of themselves as Casanovas and can be wolves in sheep's clothing, looking bland and innocent before unveiling a wide repertoire of unusual tricks in the bedroom. Both sexes with these hands love romance, dining out and visiting places of interest. They like to make themselves useful and can worm their way into the affections of others by doing so. Warm-hearted and sympathetic,

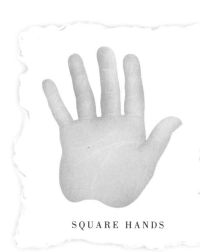

SQUARE HANDS

CONIC HANDS

LONG HANDS

they love to talk about love. You will find many of these hands in the nursing, teaching and caring professions.

Subjects with long hands are very romantic. Love begins in the mind with them and they must have mental stimulation and shared interests before they can form a relationship. They need a calm atmosphere for love-making, otherwise they can become over-anxious and tense; this is especially the case if a network of fine lines is visible on the palm.

Fingers

The hands play a big part in love-making, so let us look at them in more detail.

Strong fingers lead to vigorous, energetic love-making, especially if the mount of Venus is full.

People with short fingers lack confidence. They want to try everything but they may not have the confidence to ask for what they want nor the kind of sophistication that will get them where they want to be. These types can be clumsy, fussy or repressed and restrictive in their thinking. Small, fat hands belong on very sensual types who are also childish and have a tendency to rush partners into situations. A more relaxed and laid back attitude is needed if they are not to experience failure in one relationship after another. These subjects may ask a partner to marry them or even to have a baby with them very early in the affair. Some of this may be due to genuine romantic feelings, but it can also be due to a desire to have their partner under their control.

People with longer fingers need romance in their sex lives. If there is also a long palm, they may leave their partners wondering if they are ever going to get on with anything. Women with long, delicate hands seem to go off their partners fairly quickly, possibly because they are looking for perfection and find it hard to adapt to reality. They need romance and sex. If the mount of Venus is cramped, they may prefer a mental to a physical attachment.

Men with long, fine, hard, slightly bony hands and flat mounts are not relaters and can be dangerous Don Giovanni types. They are wrapped up in their business interests or hobbies and not at all interested in the give and take of a committed relationship. Tremendous flirts, terrifically clever in bed, but hard to pin down or have any kind of relationship with, these men make a very successful job of confusing the women they choose to

LONG FINGERS

destroy. They seem to be terrifically passionate and deeply interested at the start of a new affair. They are attractive and friendly and they know how to flatter and to focus deeply on a victim, so that she is head over heels and learning lessons of debauchery before she knows what has hit her. In actual fact, these men don't like touching, showing affection or even being especially close to their girlfriends. It is quite possible for them to make spine-tingling love, wash, dress, leave the scene and forget all about the woman before crossing the doorstep!

Oddly enough, subjects of both sexes with hands like these can be great in relationships that don't involve romantic love or sex. They make good friends and advisors and can be extremely loving parents. All the listening, affection and compassion that their lovers would like to experience with them seem to be reserved for their friends and their children. Sexual situations bring out the worst in them, possibly even turning them to verbal or physical violence. It is best to be a pal of these subjects rather than a lover, but even then they can take liberties and surprise you with their audacity.

Very weak fingers can denote fear of sex.

A long palm with short fingers denotes a subject who can be an excellent lover and partner as long as he or she doesn't plunge into the relationship too deeply, too quickly. This type can lose all sense of proportion in relationships – this is especially the case if the subject has arch or tented arch formations on the fingertips. People with long fingers coupled with a shorter palm possess the energy and enterprise to be excellent lovers,

LONG PALM, SHORT FINGERS

especially if the head line slopes downwards slightly.

Subjects with droplets on their fingertips love to touch and to be touched. They touch people of both sexes in a totally innocent way while in general conversation. In sexual situations, they love to be stroked and to massage or stroke a partner in return. Such subjects may take up massage or aromatherapy professionally. Those who don't get enough touching or stroking in their own lives will seek out massage for themselves or they may take it up in an uncon-

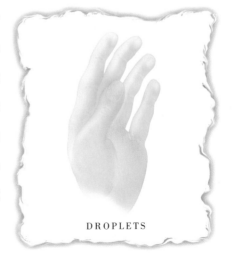

SHORT PALM, LONG FINGERS

scious need to touch and handle others. This has nothing overtly to do with sex, but it does point to a deficiency of touching and being touched.

If the Apollo finger is long, the subject is likely to be quite vulnerable and apt to fall in love too easily. If the Mercury finger is long and the heart line is low, they love to talk about sex and can get off on "talk dirty" situations. If both of these fingers are long, the head line swoops downwards and the heart line is long and deeply curved, the subject will enjoy a lively and rewarding fantasy life.

DROPLETS

The back of the hand

Turn your subject's hand over and look at the back of it. If the hand is chubby and has dimples over the knuckles, the subject shows less finesse in lovemaking. Such subjects are hard-working, warm-hearted and very fond of the opposite sex. They tend to choose similar types to themselves and to mingle with them socially. They love sex just

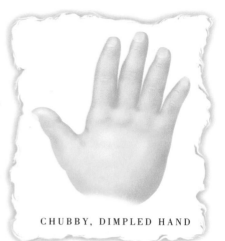

CHUBBY, DIMPLED HAND

for fun but can be selfish, thoughtless and more tuned in to their own needs than those of any partner. With thick fingers, this would be a clumsy lover. With a short thumb, the subject doesn't understand the needs and emotions of a partner. If the nails are short, fan-shaped or square at the base, look for a quick temper and a tendency to become frustrated easily.

When the hands are veined on the back, the subject is sensitive. The hands are sensitive to touch, so touch and sensitivity in love-making becomes important, even more so if there are slight droplets on the finger-tips. Sex may not be exciting as with a more passionate type but the subject is romantic, especially if the fingers are long. If the thumb and Jupiter finger are over-developed, the subject will tend to put work before the partner, maybe just using them for sex.

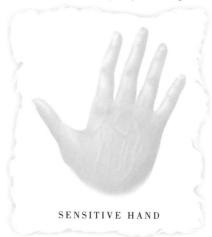

SENSITIVE HAND

We ought to say a word or two about gay relationships. Gay people have the same hands as straight ones so all our comments about love and sex apply in the same way. However, if the subject is confused about his sexuality, there will be a line peeling down from the heart line to join the head or life line. In straight or gay people, such a line can indicate childhood abuse.

THE SPIRITUAL SIDE OF LIFE

*T*he term spiritual is often misunderstood as something unconnected to the everyday or the lives of ordinary people. This is true in the sense that we are not obviously dependent on a spiritual dimension to meet our basic needs and that the increasingly material nature of life encourages us to relate only to things we can see or explain rationally.

Consideration of matters relating to that deeper intuition within us, which we shall call the spirit, tend to be forgotten. Fortunately for us, though, spiritualization occurs whether we are aware of it or not. Just as our brain-equipped physical selves learn how to drive, to use computers or to speak different languages, so our spirits learn and develop, but in a non-material dimension. Our spirits learn through the auras of other people.

The concept of the aura is well known from Eastern religions. Put simply, the aura, which each of us has, is the field of energy around us and is pure spirit. The aura can have a bearing on our lives without our knowing. For example, there are occasions when we meet a person with whom we have an instant rapport but whom we know we have not met before physically. If you were to question this soul-mate you might find that years before you had both been in the same place where your auras communicated without either of you being aware of their meeting.

Healing

Indicators of the extent to which we are in touch with our inner selves show in the hands. These signs are most marked in people who are highly spiritualized. If you get the chance to watch a spiritual healer at close quarters, using his energies to give healing to a sick person, take a look at his hands immediately after he has finished. You may notice a brown shadow visible under the health line. The appearance of this shadow, which will disappear after a few minutes, is caused by the life force flowing up this line.

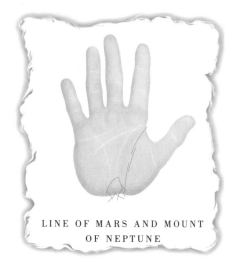

LINE OF MARS AND MOUNT
OF NEPTUNE

The mount of Neptune is the bridge between our conscious (outer) and our unconscious (inner) selves. The healer has to cross this divide, by opening up the chakras (energy centres) situated between the top of the head and the base of the spine and letting the energy flow. The effects of this in action can be tracked in microcosm on the hand. If you look at the illustration of the Kanda Ethereal Triangle, you will see how Neptune corresponds to the lower end of the spinal column (the seat of healing energy) and links with the line of Mars, the line of health and the life line (this time representing the spinal cord) to form a triangle of energy.

Comparatively few people have developed to this level of intuition and awareness. However, as a general rule, any small branch line coming off the life line and connecting with the mount of Neptune signifies some degree of bridging between the inner and outer self. Those of you inter-

KANDA ETHEREAL TRIANGLE

ested in astrology will know that Neptune is associated with the brain and nervous system. Its importance in healing, meditation and all levels of consciousness is explained by its being a relay centre for the transmission of sensory information.

HEALING STRIATA ON THE MOUNT OF MERCURY

LOCATION ON THE MOUNT OF MERCURY	THE AREAS OF LIFE THAT WILL PREDOMINATE
PERCUSSION SIDE	*Emotions; marriage, children, and caring for children*
BASE OF MERCURY	*Communication, relating, teaching, psychism and clairvoyance*
APOLLO SIDE	*Home, caring for others, healing; the outside world*
HEART LINE SIDE	*Whole-hearted dedication to work; being in charge*

The line of Mars

The line of Mars may or may not be apparent on the hand. Its presence signifies protection in life and health. If you stray too far from your true spiritual path, you may find situations developing that will bring you up short or prevent you from continuing too far in the wrong direction. If the line flows back into the mount of Neptune, the subject will have an inner awareness of this path and will tend to follow it.

Healing striata

The healing striata are situated on the mount of Mercury. Striata on the major hand show the influence of other auras and how this affects us. Striata on the minor hand show our inner self and how we really want to be. The absence of healing striata denote a young soul who has yet to find its incarnated path. If the health line reaches the mount of Mercury and then fades away, the subject is apprehensive about talking to or communicating with others.

HEALING STRIATA

Three slightly diagonal lines are the most common type of healing or medical striata. One line in this area indicates that the subject can work alone. One, two, three or four lines signify someone who works one-to-one with people.

The presence of many fine lines suggests working in a group. A line that touches the heart line and another that touches the lower end of the finger mean that the subject is a teacher and a communicator. If a line reaches into the corner of the Mercury finger, the subject is psychic.

A long fork on the Apollo side suggests that the subject saves people. This person may be a nurse in casualty or intensive care, a surgeon or a healer.

A long line with a "Y" formation on the top belongs on the hands of those who work with terminally ill people. Their job is, unconsciously perhaps, to "lift souls", that is to help them pass from this world to the next. This "Y" formation can be found on the hands of, for example, hospice staff.

A long fork on the percussion side, near the attachment lines, shows that the subject cares for children. He or she may foster, adopt or work with children.

THE SPIRITUAL ASPECTS OF LIZ

On this handprint you can clearly see all the lines referred to in this chapter. You'll notice that the healing striata is on the Apollo side, that concerned with the outside world. There is only one line, indicating that the subject works best on a one-to-one basis with people. She can be self-sufficient with few but well-selected, long-lasting friends.

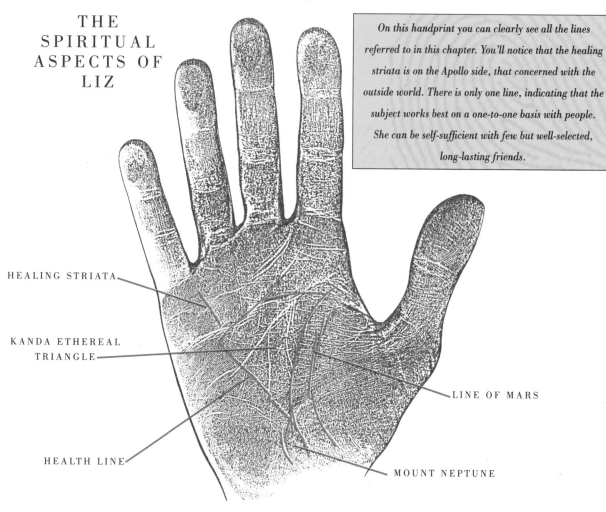

HEALING STRIATA

KANDA ETHEREAL TRIANGLE

LINE OF MARS

HEALTH LINE

MOUNT NEPTUNE

General signs of psychism

Apart from the presence of a health line and the healing striata, there are other signs that point to intuition and possible psychism. If you have any of the following on your hand, your intuition will be strong. If you have a number of them, you will probably be psychic.

SIGNS OF INTUITION AND PSYCHISM ON THE HAND

A full mount of Neptune, linking the conscious and unconscious mind
A curved line of intuition
A long sloping head line
A looped skin ridge pattern below the head line
A double loop or whorl on the Jupiter finger or the thumb
"Busy" hands rather than "empty" ones

HEALTH MATTERS

Always remember that health and healing are the realms of experts, so be careful when applying the information given in this section. Don't upset yourself or others unnecessarily. A judicious warning, though, may help to solve a potential problem before it actually appears. The hands, being a very sensitive part of the body, show past, present and future health problems very clearly.

Temperature

Hot and sweaty hands may point to thyroid or glandular problems, but some people just have hands like that. Hot and dry hands are more likely to denote a fever, high blood pressure or a kidney problem. Cold hands indicate shock or the onset of a fever. Cold, clammy hands can indicate liver problems or circulatory trouble. If the sides of the fingers feel cooler than the tops and bottoms, or different in some other way, angina or some similar illness may be indicated.

Appearance

If the hands are very soft, the subject may be elderly and losing strength or they may be young but sick. Vegetarians may have hands that are softer than usual, possibly due to a shortage of protein. Women's hands become soft during pregnancy. If the skin is satiny, smooth and shiny, the thyroid gland may be overactive. In this case, ask your subject to spread his hands and then check for a tremor.

Hands should have a normal healthy colour compatible with the skin tone of the subject. If they are pale, the circulation is not good and if the nails stay pale for a while after they have been pressed, the subject is anaemic. If you suspect anaemia, check the nails because they will be dry, pale and brittle and the third phalange of the fingers will be thin and wasted in appearance.

Blue/grey fingers denote heart and artery problems, while yellow ones signify jaundice. Red hands may indicate hormone problems, high blood pressure or glandular trouble. Smokers often have a red patch over the mounts of Luna and upper Mars. Red patches may indicate anger or worry and in this case, look at the area of the hand to judge what it is that is making the subject angry or worried. In sufferers from a condition called Raynaud's disease, the hands and feet become cold and blue from spasms of the blood vessels.

When the weather is cold, some people lose the circulation in their fingers and toes completely. The blood vessels constrict and the fingers lose all sensation for a while. This syndrome is aggravated by smoking but it is often caused by drugs such as beta-blockers or some medications for asthma or migraine. A wrinkled, bent-under and deformed ring finger and disturbances on the Apollo area of the hand denote liver damage from years of heavy drinking. (Don't confuse this with trigger finger, which is caused by a shorten-ing of the tendon in the palm which pulls one of the fingers inwards.)

A single crease across the palms is supposed to be an indication of Downs syndrome and is considered to be a way of diagnosing it in babies. This is incorrect. Downs children don't have this lateral crease on the hands; they have it on the feet. On the feet of a Downs syndrome child, the big toe is set apart from the others and there is a deep crease across the sole. The hands are rounded and elemental, with short fingers spread well apart. There may be no attachment lines, fate lines or much else but the three major lines are marked as usual.

Abnormally large hands and feet suggest too much growth hormone. Long thick fingers with loose flexible joints indicate Marfan's syndrome, a rare inherited disorder of the collagen tissue.

Very creased and old-looking hands are often an indication of asthma.

Fingertips

In elderly people, the fingertips become soft and wrinkled. In the week or so before someone dies of natural causes, the fingertips begin to lose their colour and turn grey. Hormone activity is shown by small horizontal creases on the fingertips. A recent interesting discovery is that people who have whorl markings on their fingertips are likely to develop high blood pressure.

Fingernails

The fingernails take from six to eight months to grow out and are therefore an excellent indicator of the state of a subject's health at the time of a reading. It doesn't take a genius to work out that bitten nails are a sign of nerves. Such people lack self-confidence and may either be quiet and shy or

Ailments That Show In The Fingernails

An amazing number of ailments can be spotted from the fingernails, as this list shows. If a physical or emotional shock occurs or if the subject is ill, there will be dents called Beau's lines across the nails.

ANAEMIA: *Pale nails that remain white for a while after being pressed. Dry brittle nails. In severe cases, dished nails that could hold a drop of water; this condition is called koilonychia.*

HEART/CIRCULATION: *Blue finger ends, mauve nails. Differences in temperature in different areas of the hand and the fingers.*

FUNGAL INFECTION: *Black or green nails. Deformed nails. This takes a six-month or year-long course of anti-fungal tablets to eradicate.*

DEFICIENCIES: *White flecks could be the result of too vigorous manicuring that damages the nail that is still developing under the cuticle. They could also be caused by zinc or calcium deficiency or slight deficiency of vitamins A and D.*

HEART/LUNG DISEASE, GRAVES' DISEASE, CYANOTIC HEART DISEASE, CIRRHOSIS OF THE LIVER, CROHN'S DISEASE: *Known as Hypocratic or watchglass nails, these are clubbed and raised from the surface of the finger.*

LUNG DISEASE AND FLUID RETENTION IN THE LEGS: *Yellow nails.*

KIDNEY DISEASE: *Pure white nails that signify a serious fall in protein in the body. Also nails that are yellow near the cuticle and brown at the tip end.*

BAD DIET, CALCIUM DEFICIENCY: *Very brittle nails, white marks, nails that curl under.*

BLEEDING DISORDERS: *Black marks that are actually flecks of dried blood growing into the nail. If there is a black round spot under the nail that has not been caused by the subject damaging his finger, suggest that he goes to a doctor as this could be the start of melanoma (skin cancer).*

DRUG THERAPY: *Chemotherapy and AZT (a drug taken by HIV sufferers) can leave black marks.*

RHEUMATOID ARTHRITIS, SLIPPED DISCS, BONE PROBLEMS: *Longitudinal ridging and "beading". Many people over the age of 40 have this as part of the ageing process. One nail with a deep longitudinal ridge shows some kind of damage to a bone or the ligaments, tendons or cartilage. It is worth asking your subject if he has suffered any spinal or bone damage in the past, because you will be able to confirm this from the nails. Try your skills by telling him what you see before asking for confirmation. If there is beading, ridging or one strong ridge on the thumb or Jupiter nail, the head and spine will be affected; if on the Saturn nail, the spine, ribs and upper pelvis; if on Apollo, the legs, arms, shoulders and hips; if on Mercury, the hands, ankles and feet.*

PSORIASIS, ALOPECIA AND ECZEMA: *Pitting and, in the case of psoriasis, a messy overgrowth of skin on either side of the nails. Eczema patches are interesting in themselves to a palmist because the area of the hand they cover can reveal what is on the subject's mind.*

STOMACH, BLADDER, KIDNEY, PANCREATIC OR GLANDULAR PROBLEMS: *Tiny nails that look as if they are not properly fixed in place.*

NUTRITIONAL DEFICIENCIES, BRAIN DEFICIENCIES: *Spoon-shaped nails.*

nervous and talkative; they feel ineffectual and not in control of their lives.

Nails should be a healthy pink colour, suggesting that there is plenty of oxygen reaching the extremities. Chipped and broken nails are obviously the result of working with the hands or using chemicals. Women usually take good care of their nails whatever work they do, so if you come across one who doesn't, consider her mental condition because something may be wrong.

The moons

If the moons suddenly change in character, becoming very large or disappearing altogether,

there will be heart problems. If they have always been odd, there is nothing to worry about – it is sudden changes that matter.

What the Lines Reveal: From Major to Minor

Head line

Accidents to the head are shown by a break on the head line. A square formation over such a break shows a degree of protection. Mental problems are found when the head line is very disturbed or islanded. A weird formation at the end of the head

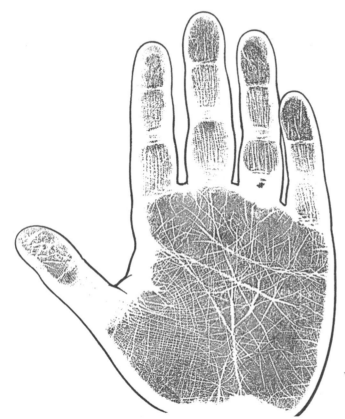

> **Sugar-tong formation**
> *This small formation found on the percussion side of the hand takes its name from its shape and is associated with insomnia. Notice its close proximity to the head line which it looks as though it is pinching or nipping, preventing the subject from resting. The sugar tong is usually found on a full hand where the lines form many squares and triangles. Sleeplessness can be due to a variety of causes. In this subject it may be an allergy to certain foods or drugs, as indicated by the via lasciva touching the life line.*

SUGAR TONG

VIA LASCIVA

line, such as a pair of sugar tongs or a crab's claw, shows that the subject isn't sleeping too well. He may have too much on his mind to be able to relax properly. A chained head line suggests feeble-mindedness. A tasselled end to the head line suggests senility or mental fatigue, or a condition connected with the head, such as blindness or deafness. Fine lines forming a grille pattern in the plain of Mars under the head line denote a nervous stomach.

Heart line

If the heart line in the area of the mount of Mercury is hard to the touch, there is high blood pressure or heart trouble. Feathering on this line under the mount of Mercury suggests possible angina or some problem with the myocardium. Islands near this area also show stress to the heart, while dots here suggest an impending heart attack. If the dot is enclosed by a circle, the subject is likely to be saved from this fate in the nick of time. Islands on the line around the Mercury/Apollo area suggest dental, mouth, throat or lung problems. If you ask your subject to flex

his hand and you find deep, bluish dips or sunken sections on the heart line, there will be some kind of lung damage in evidence. We have both seen this on the hands of people who have had tuberculosis.

A feathered or flaky heart line denotes a short-age of a trace element such as potassium. If you see this formation on a hand, suggest that your subject eats bananas or tomatoes to raise his potassium levels.

Life line

A heavily dotted life line denotes spinal disorders. If you regard the life line as a picture of the spine, you can soon work out which section is affected. Dots on the major hand denote bone and disc problems, while those on the minor hand show problems with the muscles and ligaments of the back. A group of dots close to the start of the line, just as it peels away from the head line, suggests neck disorders, while dots low down on the line denote a slipped disc, lumbago or sciatica, especially if the line pulls outward.

If the life line breaks

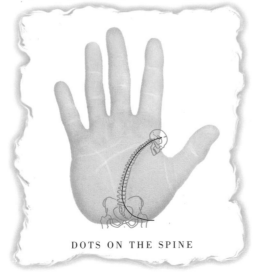

DOTS ON THE SPINE

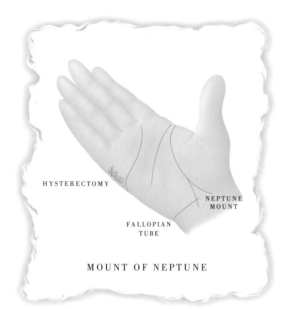

HYSTERECTOMY

NEPTUNE
MOUNT

FALLOPIAN
TUBE

MOUNT OF NEPTUNE

Attachment lines

A warty disturbance in and among the attachment lines indicates some kind of problem with the reproductive organs.

Child lines

The child lines can show losses through miscarriage and abortion. A fairly strong child line that doesn't extend as far as the attachment line can

up, becomes tasselled, islanded or weakened in any way, the subject will suffer a period of ill-health, either at the time of the reading or in the future.

Mount of Neptune

This can contain fascinating information about health. Often found here is a large, inverted "V" shape composed of the ends of various lines and a couple of stray extra ones. This "V" can be looked upon as a kind of X-ray of the female reproductive organs and any disturbances visible on it indicate problems with these organs. If one side of it is disturbed, the subject will have something wrong with an ovary, a Fallopian tube or the side of the uterus itself. If the whole area is shiny or odd-looking, your subject may have had a hysterectomy. A grille over the attachment lines also shows hysterectomy.

CHILD LINES

ATTACHMENT LINES

indicate a miscarriage. Wavy and islanded lines and other oddities can indicate abortion. Islanded lines or lines with feathers or "V" formations at their ends can indicate worry over children who are sick or misbehaving.

Health line

In a woman's hand, islands, dots and so on close to the lower end of the health line can indicate difficulty in pregnancy and birth. Dots on the health line signify an acute problem of some kind, such as kidney stones. Dots on the health line come and go with changes in the condition of the subject's health.

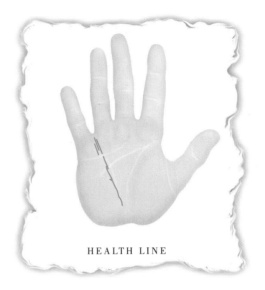

HEALTH LINE

Via lasciva

Disturbances on the via lasciva show a sensitivity to drugs and a tendency towards allergies.

PALM WATCH

◁ *If the skin ridges on the hand are broken down into "strings of pearls", the subject may be suffering from alcoholism or drug addiction.*

◁ *People who work with the sick or as counsellors will find their health lines glowing redly while they are working and for a little while after they have finished.*

◁ *If you are looking at the hand of a young, apparently healthy woman and you see a build-up of fine lines and a bit of redness in this area, she is pregnant. On a man's hands, the same thing denotes sexual frustration!*

◁ *Islands under Saturn can indicate deafness.*

◁ *Faded or blank patches on any of the lines suggest periods of ill health and these will mend themselves when the subject recovers.*

◁ *A fanning out of fine lines or a grille effect low down on the hand between the fate line and the mount of Pluto suggest diabetes. Acute diabetes will show up with broken, overlapping lines.*

TALENTS, ABILITIES AND CAREERS

There are many pointers that can help someone choose their career destiny. In this chapter you will find a range of career paths and the palmistry characteristics associated with each. Palmistry is not an exact science and we can only make suggestions as to the direction in which your interests and aptitudes may take you. We provide a multitude of possibilities for you to consider. In addition to using the examples here to answer a few questions you may have about your own career destiny, we suggest that you see if you can detect any similarities between the characteristics given with those you find on the hands of people you know.

However, before looking at these examples, here are some general tips on what the major lines and hand shapes can reveal about this aspect of our lives.

The progress of a career on the lines

Remember to study the fate line to see when and how the subject may change her life and in what direction. If the fate line rises from the life line, the subject will find her own way into the right kind of career for her. This may happen later rather than sooner after a period of time in the wrong job. If you find such a line, remember to check the life line, because this will reinforce the idea of a change of direction. If the fate line doesn't appear on the hand until after the age of 30, it will take the subject some time before she finds a job that suits her.

Self-employment is signalled by a doubling or fragmenting of the line, while a sudden job change is signalled by a fork that temporarily ends the line. Study the line to see if it jumps to the thumb side, suggesting a time of worldly achievement, or if it jumps towards the percussion side, suggesting a time away from the rat race.

The life line shows changes in location that may have something to do with the subject's career and lifestyle in general. A spreading out of the life line towards the centre of the hand is a good indication of efforts being made in a career and of material success.

The head line is a terrific indicator of career matters. If it is smooth and undisturbed, the subject's working life will be mundane and straightforward. If the line is wavy, there will be ups and downs to be lived through. Any breaks, blocking lines or disturbances on the line indicate setbacks of various kinds. A branch that rises from the head line suggests a successful new start, while a falling line denotes giving something up. Forks denote a job with plenty of variety or a variety of jobs during the subject's life. Too many forks can indicate too many interests, while a main line with a few fine lines branching off it shows a rounded personality who has a job that pays the bills but maintains plenty of outside interests. An island on the head line denotes a time of struggle and confusion. A square suggests that the subject is stuck in a job that is restrictive and frustrating but may also represent security.

Hand shapes and personality types

Above all, bear in mind the general shape of the hand. Is is practical and square, artistic and long, athletic and strong, lazy and soft, inventive and spatulate, sociable and rounded, or intellectual and delicate? Is the head line long or short, showing how inclined the subject is to use her mind or not? Does it slope, showing imagination and creativity, or is it straight, suggesting mathematical ability? Are any of the fingers very long? Is the fate line strong, suggesting a set path in life, or does it fragment, suggesting a life filled with variety?

For a moment consider all the different types of personalities and talents involved directly and indirectly in the manufacture of just one household item. In terms of the jobs they do, they may range from inventors, designers and sales and marketing executives to accountants, production workers, personnel managers, security staff and cleaners. It may not take a long, artistic, sensitive hand to clean the factory floors, but someone with this type of hand may be performing that task to help her pay her way while she is composing something wonderful.

Among the fascinating aspects of collecting the prints needed for this book have been the unexpected similarities we have found in some of the hands. All the subjects involved in engineering, for example, had straight, low heart lines with heavy flakes extending to the start of the head and life lines. A palmist would normally assume that such a subject had had a very difficult childhood or was worried about his sexuality. In fact, all these men married early and were keen to establish a stable family unit before going on to concentrate on their careers. This story is a good reminder of the many variations from accepted palmistry "norms" that may be discovered.

We will now take a look at different personality types and their aptitude for work and play.

The practical type

Practical people have square hands, and the more solid the appearance of the hand the greater is the degree of practicality. A square palm or square fingertips will add practicality to an otherwise inventive, sporty or artistic type of person. A square palm with fingertips that are rounded suggests a sociable person with a strong streak of common sense. Even a long and quite artistic hand can have a squareish palm, showing the ability to bring creative ideas to fruition. Square fingertips add a touch of caution, plus financial or technical ability, to an athletic, creative or out-going personality. The key idea to bear in mind is that any squareness adds common sense and the ability to finish the job.

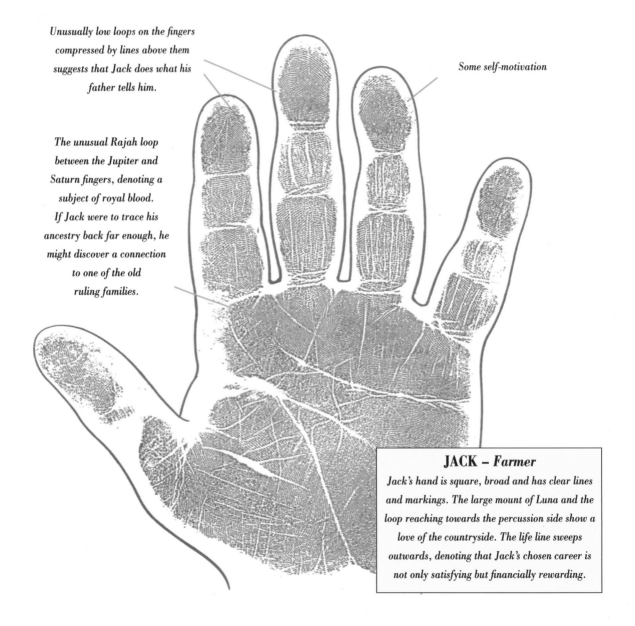

Unusually low loops on the fingers compressed by lines above them suggests that Jack does what his father tells him.

The unusual Rajah loop between the Jupiter and Saturn fingers, denoting a subject of royal blood. If Jack were to trace his ancestry back far enough, he might discover a connection to one of the old ruling families.

Some self-motivation

JACK – Farmer

Jack's hand is square, broad and has clear lines and markings. The large mount of Luna and the loop reaching towards the percussion side show a love of the countryside. The life line sweeps outwards, denoting that Jack's chosen career is not only satisfying but financially rewarding.

CAREER PATHS	CHARACTERISTICS
FARM-WORKER	*Thick, square hand, rounded or square fingertips*
FARM OWNER	*Could have rounded hand with squarish palm. Could have square palm with spatulate fingers*
BUILDER	*Square hand, rather bony, rounded or spatulate fingertips, sloping head line*
COOK	*Plump, square hand, could have rounded fingertips*
DRIVER	*Square, hard hands*
HAIRDRESSER	*Square palm, thin hand, long fingers, curved head line. Apollo finger long and with a whorl or peacock's eye*

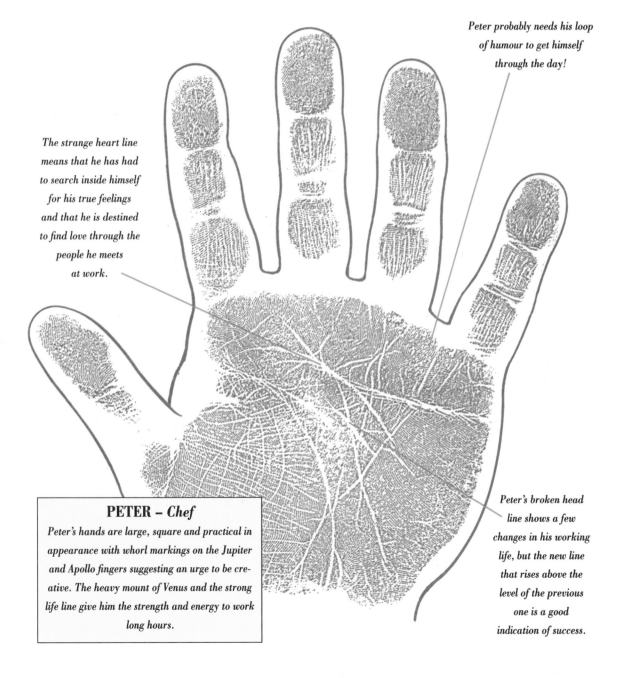

Peter probably needs his loop of humour to get himself through the day!

The strange heart line means that he has had to search inside himself for his true feelings and that he is destined to find love through the people he meets at work.

PETER – *Chef*

Peter's hands are large, square and practical in appearance with whorl markings on the Jupiter and Apollo fingers suggesting an urge to be creative. The heavy mount of Venus and the strong life line give him the strength and energy to work long hours.

Peter's broken head line shows a few changes in his working life, but the new line that rises above the level of the previous one is a good indication of success.

Flexible skills

Flexibility in the hand denotes a flexible approach to life. People with rounded and flexible hands are usually amiable types who often get on in their careers because of their natural inter-personal skills. They can do well in a variety of jobs. Plenty of loop markings on the fingertips in addition to flexibility in the hand denote a good teamworker.

If the fingers can be easily bent backwards, the subject can adapt to most circumstances but needs variety and is easily bored; people in the caring professions often have this characteristic. Long Mercury fingers and straightish head lines are often found in those who are used to dealing with many different kinds of people in their job, such as secretaries and telephonists.

CAREER PATHS	CHARACTERISTICS
SECRETARY, BOOKKEEPER, CLERICAL WORKER	Secretary/clerical worker could have straightish head line and conic hands, loops on fingertips, rounded nails. Bookkeeper has more delicate hands with square fingertips
MANAGER	If high-powered, fairly thick hands with heavy mounts of Venus and Luna
SHOP WORKER	Energetic hands with loops and a loop of humour
NURSE	Loop of humour, thickish hands, heart line throwing a branch to the ring of Solomon
SCHOOL WORKER	Wide fingers, practical hands but with the rounded fingers of the caring type. Heart line throws branch to Solomon
LEISURE WORKER	Rounded hands with some spatulate fingers and whorls on some fingertips.

Artistic and creative personalities

Serious professional artists usually have one of two totally different types of hand. When someone who knows nothing about hand-reading is asked what an artistic hand would look like, he or she invariably answers that the hand should be long and delicate-looking. This is half right, because many artistic people do have hands just like that. However, these hands are not the best type to have if the artist wants to reach the top of his profession. Many musicians have short and stumpy hands with fingers that resemble bunches of bananas, while many writers have small, energetic-looking hands. These hands may look completely out of place, but they show that the subject has the energy and drive to complete the processes that are involved in learning his profession and in taking him to the top. Among successful partnerships in the creative and entertainment fields, one partner will invariably have longer, more introspective and emotional hands, while the other has smaller, more energetic hands.

Some actors have big, broad, bony hands with

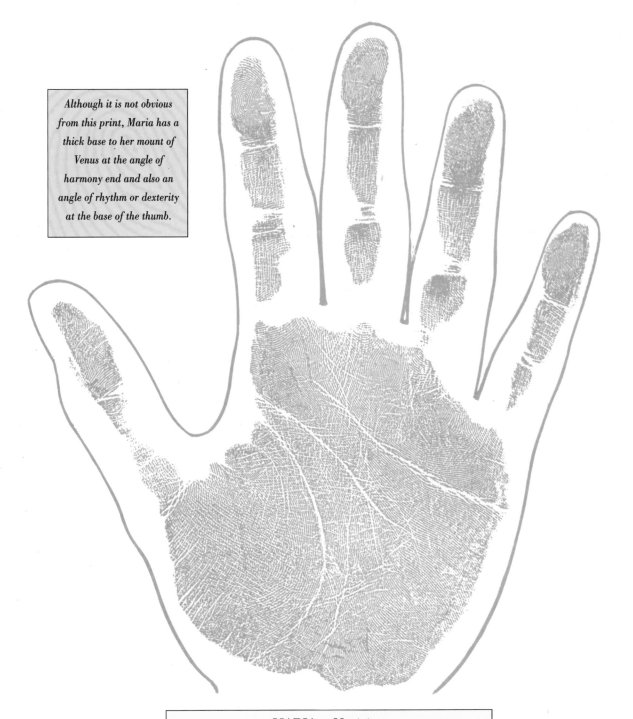

Although it is not obvious from this print, Maria has a thick base to her mount of Venus at the angle of harmony end and also an angle of rhythm or dexterity at the base of the thumb.

MARIA – *Musician*

Maria's long hand with the curved heart line and long fingers show her to have an artistic temperament. The curved percussion endows her with creativity. Her thick, strong Apollo finger and high mount of Apollo show her interest in the arts. Although musically trained, Maria also acts (note that the Jupiter, Saturn and Apollo fingers are much the same length).

a sharply outlined knuckle at the base of the thumb and a heavy turned-back thumbtip. Others have ugly, knobbly hands or strangely angular ones. The fingers form an odd alignment because the Jupiter, Saturn and Apollo fingers are almost the same length as each other, and the thumb is heavy. Next time you are watching a film with a very good-looking star in it, pay close attention to his or her hands. In comparison with the face, the hands of such stars are often amazingly ugly and, unless a manicurist has been hard at work, the fingernails can be quite offputting. Pop singers and musicians of both sexes generally have long fingers and their fingernails are more attractive.

CAREER PATHS	CHARACTERISTICS
ARTIST	Long hands or surprisingly stumpy ones. A long Apollo finger with a whorl or peacock's eye. Sloping head line
MUSICIAN	Either very long or stumpy hands. Long Apollo finger with a whorl or peacock's eye. Thick fingertips, especially the Apollo finger. Angles of dexterity and harmony emphasized
WRITER	Long Mercury and Apollo fingers and a high mount of Mercury, possibly with a cross on it. Sloping head line with forks. Loop of serious intent. Fate line throws branches to Mercury. Full mounts of Luna and Neptune
SINGER	As per musician but with high mount of Venus
ACTOR	Various shapes, ranging from large to knobbly or angular. Fingers of similar length; often unattractive nails. Large, angular thumb that turns back
FASHION DESIGNER	Long fingers, loop of style under Apollo finger, whorl or peacock's eye on Apollo finger. Sloping head line. Full mount of Luna and Neptune. Droplets on fingers
DRESSMAKER	A more square and practical hand than the designer but otherwise much the same. Droplets on fingers are a necessity here

Communicators

Communicators can be salespeople, teachers, lecturers, secretaries, shop workers and all those who deal with the public. Journalists, broadcasters or anybody else for whom communicating is a way of life come into this category. All these subjects need a long Mercury finger, preferably with a whorl or a peacock's eye on it. Also needed are a long head line, possibly forked at the end. Studious subjects have the loop of serious intent between their Saturn and Apollo fingers and knotted knuckles. Bear in mind the basic characteristics that are needed – the desire to pass on knowledge by teaching or writing, the desire to make money by selling or the desire to help people – and look at the appropriate areas.

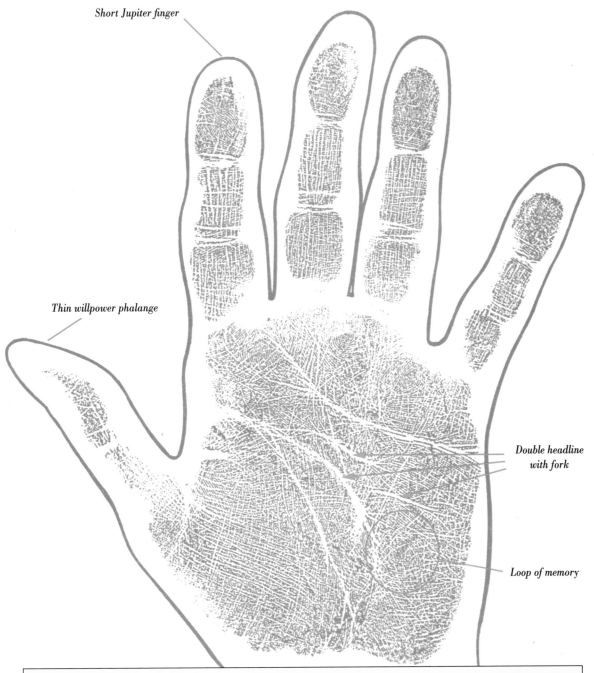

Short Jupiter finger

Thin willpower phalange

Double headline
with fork

Loop of memory

SASHA – *Writer*

Sasha is the author of numerous books on astrology, tarot and palmistry. In fact, she could write on many different subjects because of a double head line and a whorl on a long, straight Mercury finger. When the top phalange of the Saturn finger bends towards the Apollo finger, as Sasha's does, you can guarantee self-achievement. The presence of a loop of memory means that Sasha would have been suited to any profession requiring a high degree of mental application. That her life hasn't taken this direction is due to a very tied head to life line, a short Jupiter finger and a thin willpower phalange. These features show a very controlled childhood which took away confidence in those vital early years. The abundance of fine lines shows Sasha's sensitivity to others and her capacity for friendship. The loop of humour keeps Sasha going through a punishing schedule and stimulates those around her.

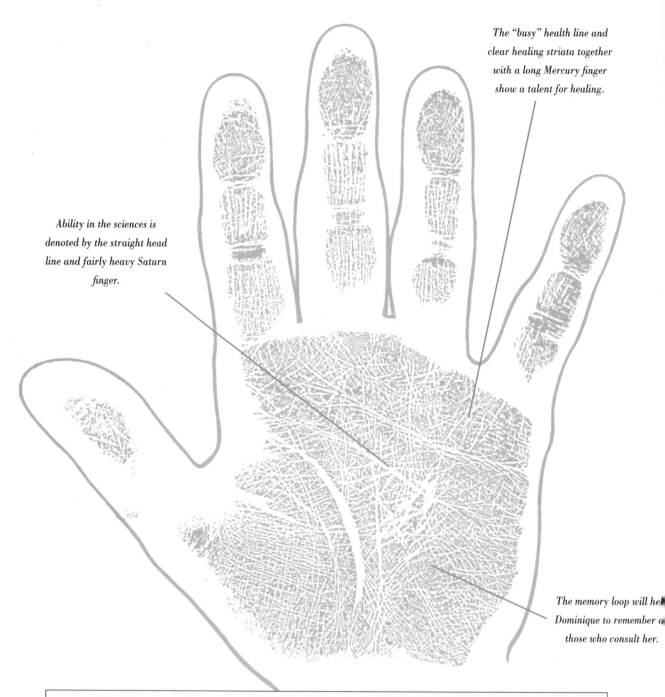

The "busy" health line and clear healing striata together with a long Mercury finger show a talent for healing.

Ability in the sciences is denoted by the straight head line and fairly heavy Saturn finger.

The memory loop will help Dominique to remember all those who consult her.

DOMINIQUE – *Doctor and herbalist*

Dominique is a doctor who is now finishing a course of study in herbalism. She has a large home and family to care for, complete with pets, and a constant stream of visitors. This busy lifestyle is shown by the wealth of lines on Dominique's hand. The vertical lines on her fingers show that her busy life is probably tiring her out at the moment.

Dominique has mentioned that she would like to do counselling work. She probably needs a stronger ring of Solomon than she has at present, but the many marks around the area of the girdle of Venus will help her to achieve this ambition. If she begins to enjoy this more intuitive and less practical work, the ring of Solomon and the curve of intuition will soon develop.

CAREER PATHS	CHARACTERISTICS
TEACHER	Can have quite bony hands with knobbly knuckles, long fingers, square palms. A square on the mount of Jupiter and a diagonal groove or line between the mounts of Mercury and Apollo. There could also be healing striata
JOURNALIST AND EDITOR	Sloping head line with forks. Straight heart line. No ring of Solomon. If reporter, flat Luna, if feature writer, higher Luna and Neptune
SALESMAN/WOMAN	Conic hands, high mount of Mercury. Long Mercury finger. Flexible fingers, spatulate or fan-shaped fingernails. A heavy mount of Venus, suggesting persistence
LECTURER	Long hands, long fingers, could be spatulate. Slightly knobbly knuckles. if successful, a full mount of Venus and Luna
PALMIST/ASTROLOGER	Long palm. Long, slightly knotted fingers, sloping head line possibly with branches. Life line ending on Neptune. Fragmented fate line
TEAMLEADERS	A loop on the Jupiter finger that enters the finger from the thumb side. Long Jupiter and Saturn fingers

A selection of professionals

Accountants, doctors, solicitors and chartered engineers are all thoughtful and intuitive people who deal with both people and technical knowledge. Such people frequently have quite beautiful hands with spatulate fingers or long hands with square fingertips. The friendly, humorous ones who are very popular with their clients have flexible and slightly rounded hands with a high mount of Mercury and a loop of humour between the Apollo and Mercury fingers. These charismatic characters may be great fun but may not necessarily be the best person to consult.

The more energetic the personality, the smaller and more compact the hand. The subject who is studious, thoughtful and inclined towards research has longer fingers, a straighter head line and more angular knuckles. He could have more to offer than his round-handed colleague in terms of the quality of his advice.

CAREER PATHS	CHARACTERISTICS
ACCOUNTANT	Slender hands with square palms and square fingertips. Straight head line. Could have a collection of small horizontal lines at the base of the Mercury finger
SOLICITOR	Similar to accountant but without the extra lines at the base of the Mercury finger
BARRISTER	Long Jupiter and Apollo fingers, sloping head line. Angular thumb
DOCTOR, THERAPIST, DENTIST	Slim, intuitive hands. Health line, healing striata, could have spatulate or square fingertips
ENGINEER	Spatulate hands with peacock's eye on Apollo or Mercury fingers. Straight head line
ADMINISTRATOR	Similar to accountant or solicitor. Healing striata showing that he deals with people

Business people

These people have many different styles of hand depending upon the talents and interests that took them into their chosen fields in the first place. The mounts of Venus and Luna are quite full and the fingers strong. If the business is confidential the subject probably has a Jupiter finger that curves towards Saturn. The head line is long and strong with a gentle slope. A salesman has good strong lines and a long Mercury finger. A caring and conscientious employer has a heart line that reaches across to the mount of Jupiter and ends in a little fork.

Large hands with large, rounded fingernails suggest an easy-going nature and a friendly personality, while small hands with small, square or spatulate nails suggest a tense, restless and ambitious nature. The second type may be hard to work for but he is more likely to remain in business when the going gets tough than his more lovable colleague.

Here are a few of the business people that we have come across. The difference in hand types is astonishing, reflecting perhaps the wide range of skills that are needed for success in the world of commerce.

CAREER PATHS	CHARACTERISTICS
PUBLISHER	Small rounded hands. Thin fingers with mixed tips: the Saturn fingertip is square while the Apollo and Mercury ones are slightly spatulate. Long, gently curving head line
INTERNATIONAL RECRUITMENT CONSULTANT	Long but powerful bony hands with heavy mounts of Venus and Luna. Long, curving head line
DIRECTOR OF AN ENGINEERING COMPANY	Short, square hands with spatulate fingertips. Full mounts, especially Mercury and Venus. Long, strong lines and a strong thumb with a heavy willpower phalange
COMPANY DIRECTOR OF A GROUP OF NURSERY SCHOOLS	Long hands with long palms. Long, forked head line. Strong Saturn finger, ring of Solomon with a branch from the heart line running into it. Healing striata and health line
MANAGING DIRECTOR OF A SOFTWARE COMPANY	Small, hard hands with large but flat mounts with long, deep, strong lines. Square fingertips with a money-maker line (see page 148)
COMPANY DIRECTOR OF AN INTERNATIONAL ASTROLOGY SOFTWARE COMPANY	Long, slender, extremely beautiful hands with a square palm. The spiritual kanda ethereal triangle. Forked head line, spatulate Apollo fingers, long Mercury fingers. Large but flat Venus and Luna areas

Sport

Logic says that sporty people should have hands that are wide at the base with a heavy thumb and a generally strong, energetic look about them, but this is not always the case; many of these subjects have quite delicate hands. The mental effort required to take them to the top is a far more important factor than the physical one. The same can be said for dancers and acrobats, both of whom can have very delicate hands with long fingers.

The straight head line with its two upward hooks at the end show that Martin's business ventures will be successful. The chances are that overseas connections will aid this success. The geographical areas that relate to the head line are the United States and Canada.

Note the unusually clear cross on the mount of Mercury. Computer-literate people usually have a cross in this area. This example is exceptionally clear.

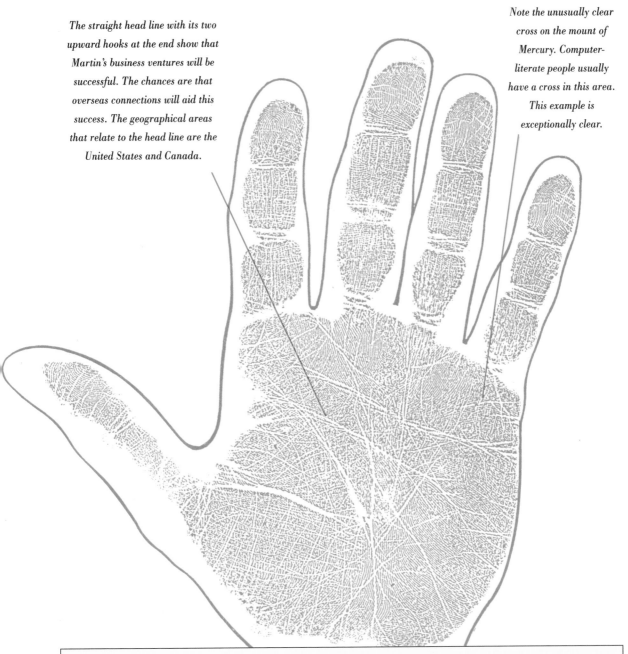

MARTIN – *Olympic sports champion and company director*

We have decided to use this versatile and interesting man to serve two categories: business and sport. Martin was a member of the USA Olympic fencing squad in Munich in 1972. He still fences competitively. For many years, Martin has run a successful company dealing in providing software for the astrology trade.

You might expect a successful sportsman to have a broad hand with a heavy angle at the base of the thumb. Martin's hand, however, is long and slender with a long, creative Apollo finger. The strong thumb and the whorl on the Jupiter finger endow willpower and the kind of competitiveness that won't allow much to stand in his way.

Martin's unusually strong and straight Apollo line, rising as it does from a branch of his fate line at around the age of 24, suggests success throughout life, either as a sportsman or as an entrepreneur.

HANDS THAT MAKE MONEY

When looking at money on a hand, you must study the motivation factors behind the subject's ambitions and goal orientation. There may be a burning desire to make a success of a business without money itself being a priority. In this case, talent, creativity and energy come into the picture as much as materialism. On the other hand, there may be a desire for money that overrides everything else. Some people obtain money without working for it, by inheriting it, marrying it or winning it. All this will be covered here, but we start with the hands most likely to be found among successful business people.

What moneymaking hands look like

As always, look first at the shape and general appearance of the hands. If the fingers are blunt, shortish and strong, the subject is materially motivated. The longer the fingers, the more creative and less materially motivated the personality. Now look at the back of the hand. If this is plump and you cannot see any veins protruding, the subject will be uninterested in the welfare of colleagues or others who are around him. This subject considers tender feelings to be a drawback in business. If the hand is finer and the veins protrude, the subject is creative and therefore feelings and inspiration would be expressed as part of his business life.

A longer, more delicate hand suggests that the subject has turned a talent or skill to advantage by making it her business. The thicker, stronger type of hand belongs to someone who is destined to be in business in some way or another, even if she has no special talents to take advantage of. The bony, knobbly, rather hard hand with small nails and strong lines belongs to a tough

SMOOTH FINGERS

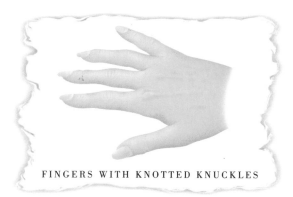

FINGERS WITH KNOTTED KNUCKLES

character who is determined to bulldoze the opposition into submission. We have come across a few very successful people who have the most beautiful and sensitive hands that you can imagine. One would assume that these people would be terrific to be around, but in fact they can be mercenary and apt to use their intellect as a weapon, not caring about the damage they do to others on their way to the top.

Mainly female go-getters

A plumpish hand with high phalanges at the base of the fingers shows a need for comfort and security, as do long, curving fingernails. There are plenty of well-dressed and successful business-women around these days and more often than not you will notice that their hands are well-kept and the nails long, curving and painted with brightly coloured nail lacquer. Another typical female business hand has a rather sharp, angular shape, a pale skin (depending upon race) and widely

spaced fingers. Knotted knuckles show that the subject pays attention to details, while a smoother hand shows that she leaves the minor daily decisions to others.

Mainly male go-getters

A thickish, strong hand belongs to a good organizer and staff manager. However, if the lower part of the hand is heavy around the mounts of Venus, Neptune, Luna and Pluto, he can be a bully. If the hand is finer but the base mount areas broad, the subject may have a cutting and sarcastic manner. A more rounded hand belongs to a subject who has a pleasant way of getting what he wants out of others.

Many businessmen have quite small, rounded hands. These subjects like variety and stimulation and require constant challenges. They treat life, including their careers, as a game and enjoy the ups and downs of business. Heavy or pudgy hands equal energy; fine ones equal inventiveness.

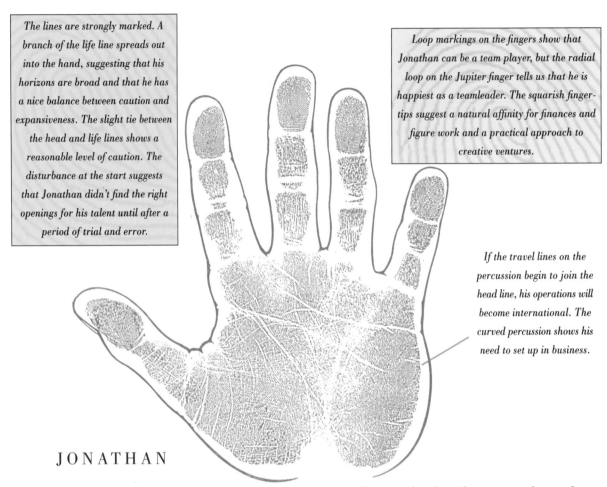

The lines are strongly marked. A branch of the life line spreads out into the hand, suggesting that his horizons are broad and that he has a nice balance between caution and expansiveness. The slight tie between the head and life lines shows a reasonable level of caution. The disturbance at the start suggests that Jonathan didn't find the right openings for his talent until after a period of trial and error.

Loop markings on the fingers show that Jonathan can be a team player, but the radial loop on the Jupiter finger tells us that he is happiest as a teamleader. The squarish finger-tips suggest a natural affinity for finances and figure work and a practical approach to creative ventures.

If the travel lines on the percussion begin to join the head line, his operations will become international. The curved percussion shows his need to set up in business.

JONATHAN

The fingers

Stiff fingers that allow no light to show between them suggest a desire to keep and control money. This will be further emphasized if the lowest phalanges of the fingers (those closest to the palm) are plump.

Prominent knuckles show a cautious attitude, while smooth fingers (see illustration on page 145) denote a more intuitive and slightly reckless attitude. If the Saturn finger is short, the subject is unrealistic and a gambler (he could be lucky much of the time, of course). Square fingertips or square nails mean that the subject can understand the intricacies of finance and accounts. Rounded fingertips or fan-shaped nails show some sales ability. This is emphasized if the Mercury finger is long and slightly bent inwards. Spatulate finger ends show a more inventive turn of mind,

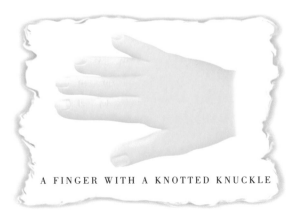

A FINGER WITH A KNOTTED KNUCKLE

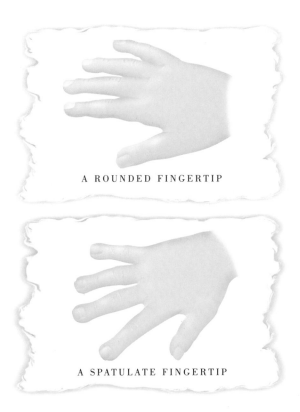

A ROUNDED FINGERTIP

A SPATULATE FINGERTIP

especially if there are whorls on some fingertips.

A long, thickish Jupiter finger denotes leadership qualities and a desire for personal achievement. If this finger curves inwards towards Saturn, the subject will be more inclined to do his own thing than to work as part of a team. This trait is emphasized if there is an arch on the fingertip. A loop that enters the Jupiter finger from the thumb side indicates a team-leader. A whorl on a strong Jupiter finger suggests that the subject will go his own way without regard to the advice of others.

A LOOP ON THE
JUPITER FINGERTIP

If the Saturn and Apollo fingers lean towards each other, the subject needs a creative and fulfilling job. If the Apollo finger is long and/or

A WHORL ON THE
JUPITER FINGERTIP

carries a whorl or peacock's eye mark on the tip, the urge for creativity is emphasized.

A strong and fairly long Mercury finger is a must for most forms of business, as this shows communication skills. A collection of fine horizontal lines at the base of the Mercury finger mean that the subject can cope with statistics. This helps with such things as cash flow charts, financial analysis and figure work of all kinds. While on the subject of statistics and finances, square fingertips and squarish nails suggest an ability to keep books and to understand the intricacies of financial matters. A cross on the mount of Mercury shows that the subject is comfortable working with computers – a necessary skill in most types of business nowadays.

A thumb that is held close to the hand denotes secretiveness and possible greed. One that is strongly made with a prominent knuckle at its base and a tip that turns back shows a need for fame as well as for fortune.

The lines

While a strong life line shows good health and the ability to work hard, a strong head line is a must for any kind of business success. If the line runs directly across the hand the subject is

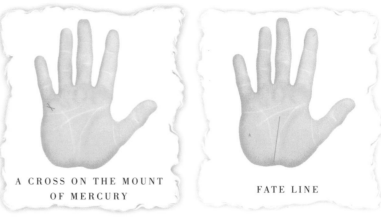

A CROSS ON THE MOUNT
OF MERCURY

FATE LINE

logical and has a head for figures, while a deeply curving line shows imaginative powers. A short head line belongs on the hand of a specialist. This is often an indication of success in business because it shows that the subject keeps his eye on the ball and is not deflected from his aims by other interests or considerations. The best head line is one that is medium in length and slightly curved. The line should have an upward branch or two and no major disturbances along its length.

A fate line that runs the length of the hand shows a lifetime devoted to duty. Whether this duty is to work, the family or something else depends on

other features on the hand. A line that rises from the life line suggests that the subject's family may help him to get started in life, but it can also denote self-motivation. A late start is shown by a fate line that gets its start in the middle or the upper areas of the hand. A clean, clear line shows an absence of challenges and is more likely to belong to someone who has a good job than to a self-employed person or a business tycoon. A disturbed fate line denotes problems; the subject's determination to overcome them is revealed if the line continues to climb up the hand after the stretch of disturbance. A ladder of success formation is evident when the fate line ends with a series of sideways jumps over to the mount of Jupiter. If the fate line is too fragmented, the subject may give up too easily. A change to self-employment is shown by a doubling or fragmenting of the fate line at the appropriate age.

One rather odd little line that is a

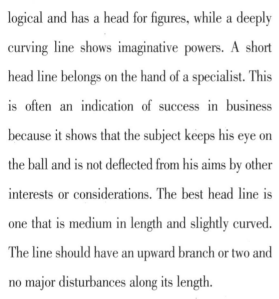

GENTLY CURVING
HEAD LINE

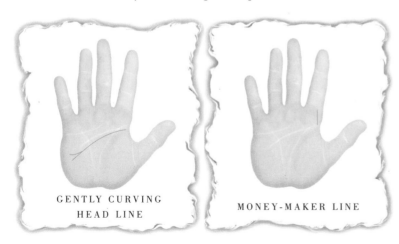

MONEY-MAKER LINE

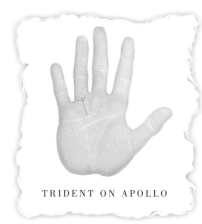

TRIDENT ON APOLLO

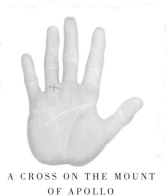

A CROSS ON THE MOUNT
OF APOLLO

fact that there is probably only one cross and it is strongly marked. In either case, the cross or crosses must be isolated from any other lines and quite distinct. A star on the Apollo mount, close to the top of the Apollo line, is another indication of fame and fortune.

lucky thing to have so far as personal finances are concerned is the money-maker line. This short, vertical line is found close to the percussion on the side of the mount of Jupiter, linking the base of the Jupiter finger to the start of the head and life line. This shows that whatever else happens in the subject's life he will always find a way of earning or obtaining money.

The second lucky sign is a trident on the mount of Apollo at the end of an Apollo line. The Apollo line need only be quite short but if the trident is present financial disasters can be averted, or if they do occur the subject will find a way of getting up on his feet once again.

Money that comes in from royalties or any other kind of work that has been done in advance is shown by one or more crosses on the mount of Apollo. The same goes for lottery, pools or other winners, except for the

A cross on the mount of Jupiter close to the end of the heart line suggests the subject marrying someone wealthy or who comes into money later.

Lines that drift over from inside the area where the life line and head line start or from inside the life line to join the fate or Apollo lines suggest inheritance of some kind. If such a line joins the fate line it is more likely to be money that is inherited, while if it joins the Apollo line the subject will inherit property. If you suspect that a property is in the offing, check the family line at the base of the thumb to see if more than one property is marked there. Don't forget the money-maker line at the side of Jupiter or the wonderful trident on Apollo. If a subject has both of these, whatever happens during his life, he will always come up smelling of crisp banknotes. An absence of lines means no striving.

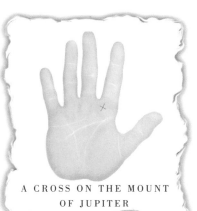

A CROSS ON THE MOUNT
OF JUPITER

PROPERTY AND YOU

*M**any of the people who consult palmists are concerned about where they are going to live and other matters related to business premises, holiday homes and even other properties that belong to their family. There are many areas of the hand that offer information on this subject, as you will discover.*

The family ring

This is read upwards from the percussion area at the base of the thumb to the area where the thumb pulls away from the hand. It is not easy to time events on this line, but if you take the middle of it to represent the age of 40, you won't go far wrong. If this ring is broken, there will be changes and possible losses in connection with property matters. Islands, discoloration and blocking lines in this area all suggest problems in connection with property.

If there are two rings, the subject will own or rent more than one property. If there is one main ring and a partial ring alongside it, there will be additional property of some sort at the appropriate stage of her life. There are many potential reasons for someone to become interested in a property extra to her home – she may inherit or have to sell up a parental home, there may be a holiday home or even a caravan and there are all kinds of business premises that can come into the picture.

If the family ring looks like a very fine-chained necklace, the subject will find it hard to put down roots or to find the right country to live in and may be the kind of person who "lives out of a suitcase".

THE FAMILY RING

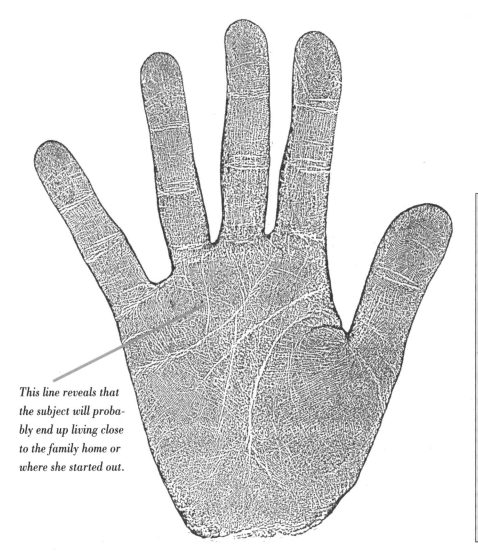

This line reveals that the subject will probably end up living close to the family home or where she started out.

The Apollo line

This line often begins somewhere in the middle of the hand and it tells you the age at which the subject becomes responsible for his own dwelling-place. It doesn't matter if the property is rented or owned, though ownership would probably show up as a stronger line than a rented flat.

Lines that break up, are islanded or otherwise disturbed show changes in connection with property. A new and stronger line that emerges after a disturbance on the line or after an influence line has crossed the Apollo line suggests a change for the better. More than one line on the mount of Apollo is a good indication of additional property. A new line closer to the Saturn mount suggests that the subject will retire close to her family, while a new line towards the Mercury mount suggests that she will choose to spend her latter days close to her friends. If the Apollo line fades from the palm on the Apollo mount, the subject could lose her home as a result of financial losses or bad business decisions. Forks on this mount suggest that she will be close to elderly relatives and that she could spend a fair bit of time in and around their property as well as her own. Additional lines close to the Apollo line or on the mount of Apollo indicate additional property. If you see this, remember to check the family ring for corroboration of your findings.

The life line

The life line gives a clue as to the location of the subject at any point in his life. Therefore, a move overseas will be indicated by the line moving out across the hand. A change of circumstances and the loss of a home will be reflected by a good deal of disturbance on the life line, which may actually peter out altogether at such a

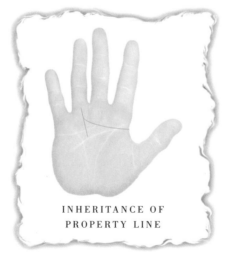

THE APOLLO LINE

INHERITANCE OF PROPERTY LINE

point in the subject's life. A new piece of life line starting up lower down on the mount of Venus will show a new start and a new home to come.

Inheritance

This aspect has also been covered on page 149, but, just for extra clarity, we'll reiterate the major pointers here. The inheritance of property is shown by an influence line that wanders over from the area where the life and head lines are close together and touches or joins a line on the mount of Apollo. (The family ring will show if you are likely to end up with an additional property that can be handed down through the family; see page 84.) A line entering from the percussion side of the hand could suggest that an outsider brings property into the subject's life. Equally, it could indicate an outsider being brought into the subject's property – a new marriage with someone from afar, perhaps? Check the lower end of the life line for additional lines on Venus to add to the evidence.

GOING PLACES

*T*ravel and geographic palmistry has only become an aspect for study relatively recently. The reason for this is that up to about 40 years ago few people regularly left their neighbourhood let alone travelled the world. Nowadays, of course, many people travel long

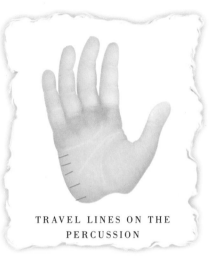

TRAVEL LINES ON THE PERCUSSION

distances without giving it a second thought. The lines that relate specifically to travel enter the hand from the percussion edge from the heart line downwards.

Travel signs

Many people have travel lines on their hands that suggest they will visit various foreign countries, but these lines don't always translate into real journeys. It would not be a surprise to find family and other contacts in foreign places or a special interest in a particular area showing up on the hand. However, it is possible to make suggestions to a person about those areas that

LIFE LINE SWEEPING OUT INTO LUNA

would be lucky or beneficial for him to visit or even to live in for a while (or they could simply be places that he would like to visit if he ever got the opportunity). They can also show a historical connection from his family's past. An example of this can be found in the hand of a friend of ours who has a strong line relating to Hong Kong. He has never been there but he comes from the famous

FATE LINE STARTING
ON LUNA

LINE ENTERING FROM
UPPER MARS

Family and friends

Important personal contacts in other countries are shown by fine lines that reach over from the percussion and touch the life line. Sometimes these lines can be seen to drag part of the life line from its course.

Jardine Matheson family who made their fortune trading in Hong Kong.

A large or high mount of Luna and a deep mount of Pluto all point to a love of travel. If the life line wanders over or throws branches to Luna, the subject will travel quite extensively and will have plenty of foreign contacts. He may even end his days in a different country. Lines that rise from the percussion, such as the fate line, the Apollo line or even a line entering the hand higher up on the mount of upper Mars, all indicate contacts with foreigners and plenty of travel during the subject's life.

Business travel

Contacts with foreigners and overseas countries are shown by lines that reach out from the head line and wrap themselves around the percussion edge. The same goes for lines that creep inwards from the percussion and touch the head line.

The areas that a person may visit or that would be beneficial for her to spend time in are marked on the percussion. The area immediately below the heart line refers to the subject's own home country. Other countries are marked downwards along the length of the percussion in order of their distance from the subject's homeland. So, for example, travel lines found closest to the heart line would suggest a link to Scandinavia, while lines close to or on Pluto would indicate a connection to South East Asia.

The Commonwealth countries of Canada, Australia and New Zealand often used to be strongly marked in subjects from the United Kingdom. Nowadays, we see Asian countries, the United States of America and, increasingly, the countries of Europe being strongly marked. This reflects the changes in the make-up and travel and business habits of many British people.

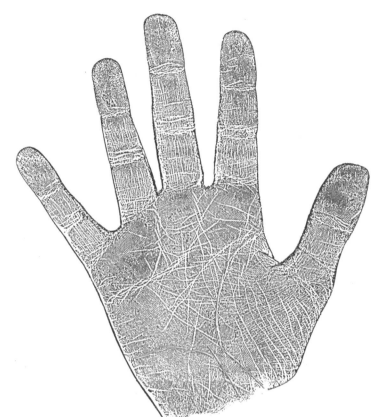

Travel types

Some people save up to have one great trip to somewhere that is different, exotic and far-flung once every few years, while others like a number of short trips. Some people find jobs that take them travelling, while others see travel as a change from their usual lives. Some travellers love aeroplanes, while others are nervous of flying. Some can take discomfort in their stride while exploring; others need five-star luxury.

Travellers can have large, small, long or short hands but they all have a large or full mount of Luna and flexible hands, often with flexible finger-tips. The luxury-loving traveller has full third phalanges on her fingers (closest to the palm). If, in addition to comfort, she likes interesting scenery and wildlife, she will have a large mount of Venus. If she loves the sea and ships, she will have a large or high mount of Luna with a loop marking on it. A long Apollo finger will lead the traveller to seek out exotic places where beautful things are made, while a long Mercury finger will lead her to seek out interesting people and information. Many travellers have fairly short Jupiter and Saturn fingers, suggesting that they are happy to take a chance on whatever comes along. Those who don't like variety, adventure or the unexpected have stiffer hands with stronger and longer Jupiter and Saturn fingers.

YOUNG AND OLD HANDS

*L*ife, it is often said, leaves its mark on each of us. We can see this in a very superficial way by looking at pictures of ourselves at various ages. You'll probably be struck by how young you looked and how strange the fashions were then. You may recall how you were feeling at the time and what was happening in your life. If Malcolm and I were to study prints of your hand taken then and now, we would see major differences between the two. Interestingly, only some of the features of the hand reflect these changes.

How the hands change

The hands of newborn babies can be large, small, broad or narrow. The hands grow in scale with other parts of the body, but their basic shape remains largely unchanged. The skin ridge patterns, which form at about eight or nine weeks of pregnancy, do not change either. The lines are a completely different matter. When we come into the world the lines on our hands are virtually identical: the basics of life, head and heart line are clearly marked, and the shape and formation of each of these lines is remarkably similar. It is only as a result of the experiences we encounter on life's journey that the myriad variations that are to be found on hands occur.

Young people

Children's hands are very difficult to read because so little information is to be found on them and what is there will quickly change. Generally speaking, a child with very few lines will develop more as time goes on, while one with a hand covered in fine lines will probably lose most of these later.

There are more similarities than differences in the hands of most youngsters, and it is only after

P A L M   W A T C H

Don't try to take a handprint from a baby or a toddler. They absolutely hate having their hands interfered with. Older children are a different matter – they love a legitimate excuse to make a mess!

Don't try to read anything into warts, red patches, discoloration or minor damage on a child's hands; none of this is important in palmistry terms.

adolescence that you can begin to draw any conclusions from their hands. Some teenagers and young adults have very young hands with few lines or marks on them, while others have hands that are almost fully developed.

While the hands of young adults show many more characteristics, they still don't have all the lines typically found in an older person. If a youngster asks if she will marry, have children, have a nice home and a good job, always give an optimistic answer, even if you don't think you can see what she is hoping to hear. There is no point in upsetting a young person unnecessarily.

Adults

By the time a subject gets into his late twenties or early thirties, you should have plenty to go on. Even here there are exceptions to this rule. A subject whose life is totally mundane won't have much showing on his hands, while a complicated and neurotic subject will have a great deal.

Older hands are great fun to read. There should be loads of information on them and, of course, the subject can verify your findings. Elderly people love having their hands read and, if you cannot find much to say about their future lives, they are usually more than happy to let you explore their past with them. Older hands are wonderful, because you can learn so much by looking at them and chatting to their owners.

Reading young and old – a comparison

We are now going to look at Malcolm's hand and compare it to his granddaughter Phoebe's. There is so much information on Malcolm's hand that it is hard to know where to start. His strongly spiritual approach to life is shown by the line of Mars and the health line which are turned into the Kanda Ethereal Triangle by a line that joins the heart line to the start of the head and life line. The large, low-slung mounts of Luna and Pluto endow Malacolm with a tremendous imagination while the sharp angle of harmony shows his love of music.

Malcolm's loop of humour and style loop show

Malcolm and Phoebe's hands: the similarities

◁ *Long fingers*

◁ *Loop of humour*

◁ *Sloping head line with fork at end*

◁ *Girdle of Venus (incomplete on Phoebe's hand), showing love of arts*

◁ *Ring of Solomon – helping others*

MALCOLM – Artist and musician

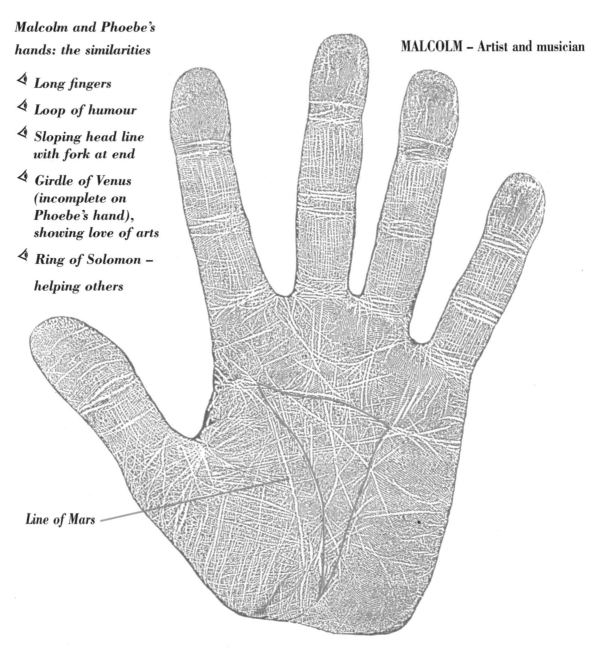

Line of Mars

his idiosyncratic approach to life. The long fingers denote attention to detail but the fact that they are smooth and not knotted tells us that he can work swiftly and decisively. The loops on all his fingers make him a cooperative colleague.

The long, deeply curving heart line shows a tremendous capacity for love; the depth, though, shows that he is fussy about the women he chooses to love! The sloping head line with its long fork at the end signifies both creative and literary ability and the upward hoop at the end of the upper branch ensures success. Note also the branch from the fate line to the mount of Mercury, a sure sign of a professional writer or illustrator.

Phoebe

Even at the tender age of four and a half the evidence is that Phoebe is a creative, caring little Piscean. The lines on her right hand are nicely rounded. Her left hand shows some inner confusion, which will probably disappear as she grows. As is the case with most children, the influence of her parents is strongly marked by the lines radiating out from the mounts of lower Mars and Venus.

The long Jupiter finger with its whorl finger-print together with the separated head and life lines show Phoebe to be a strong, independent personality. The strong apex in the skin ridge pattern on Jupiter is an early indication of success.

People from other countries or who live at a distance from her may have most influence later in life. However, much can change. The loop of humour will never change, though, and it is certain that her grandfather's wonderful sense of the ridiculous will be with her for life.

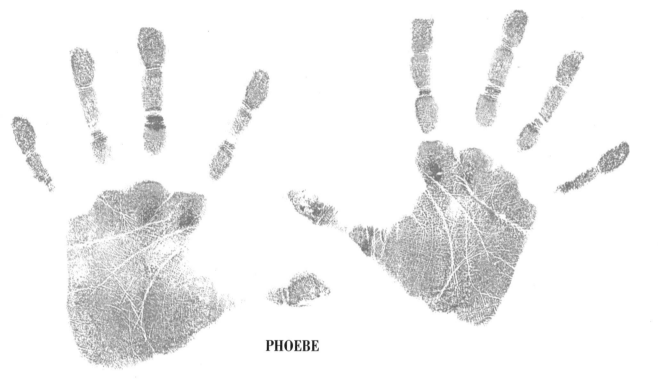

PHOEBE

LIFE LINE: *Clear; pulls towards the percussion side, denoting independence.*
HEAD LINE: *Long, curved. Good imagination; the slight upward loop near Luna shows she could be good in a creative business.*
Gap between head and heart lines; adventurous, will have a free and easy relationship with her parents.
HEART LINE: *Strong and unbroken; she should have little difficulty showing her love.*
This line will change as she grows and matures sexually.
FATE LINE: *Clear and strong with the energy moving over to the Apollo line.*
A self-achiever, she will make her mark in life; doors will open for her.

INDEX